Discovering Trinity in Disability

A Theology for Embracing Difference

MKLM Library

Myroslaw Tataryn & M

ORBIS BOOKS
Maryknoll, New York 10545

ORBIS BOOKS
Maryknoll, New York 10545

Fathers and Brothers
MARYKNOLL

Founded in 1970, Orbis Books endeavors to publish works that enlighten the mind, nourish the spirit, and challenge the conscience. The publishing arm of the Maryknoll Fathers and Brothers, Orbis seeks to explore the global dimensions of the Christian faith and mission, to invite dialogue with diverse cultures and religious traditions, and to serve the cause of reconciliation and peace. The books published reflect the views of their authors and do not represent the official position of the Maryknoll Society. To learn more about Maryknoll and Orbis Books, please visit our website at www.maryknollsociety.org.

Layout: Audrey Wells
Interior image: The Trinity of Roublev, c.1411, Andrei Roublev – Jupiter Images

Library of Congress Cataloging-in-Publication Data
Tataryn, Myroslaw I., 1956-
   Discovering Trinity in disability : a theology for embracing difference / Myroslaw Tataryn & Maria Truchan-Tataryn.
     pages cm
   Includes bibliographical references.
   ISBN 978-1-62698-037-2
   1. Church work with people with disabilities. 2. People with disabilities—Religious life. 3. Trinity. I. Title.
BV4460.T38 2013
261.8'324--dc23
                2013007704

Contents

Acknowledgements 5

Why We Wrote This Book 7

Introduction 8

1. Disabling/Disabled Communities 12

2. God—The Inclusive Community: The Trinitarian Paradigm 22

3. Deviating Bodies—Divine or Demonic: Our Hebrew
   Scriptural Tradition 25

4. The Radical Rabbi: Jesus Disables Normalcy 42

5. Embracing the Radical: Early Christian *Koinonia* 51

6. Discovering Trinity: Forming Christian Orthodoxy 54

7. Interdependent Living: Models of Christian Community 72

8. Sacred Matter: Sacraments 84

9. Mad about Miracles 90

10. Sanctuary: Abnormal Hospitality 102

11. Transfigured Corporeality: Being Icons 106

12. Discovering Trinity in Disability 116

Bibliography 124

To our daughters
Aleksandra, Anastasia, and Myroslava,
the miracles of our life.

So to come to be 'in Christ', to belong with Jesus, involves a far-reaching reconstruction of one's humanity: a liberation from servile, distorted, destructive patterns in the past, a liberation from anxious dread of God's judgement, a new identity in a community of reciprocal love and complementary service, whose potential horizons are universal.

Rowan Williams, *On Christian Theology*, 138

Acknowledgements

··

This book has existed for many years as only a thought, with little hope of materializing into text. Against all odds, words have hit paper and we feel immensely blessed to be able to acknowledge all those who have made this possible. Our sincere thanks go to Kevin Burns, formerly of Novalis, who liked the idea of linking theology and Disability Studies theory and encouraged us to write. Years later, when ownership changes and life had overtaken any chance of realizing this project, Novalis did not abandon the "thought" and continued to support it: thank you.

We are indebted to the countless people throughout Canada who have touched our lives with their unflagging dedication to their disabled family members.[1] We are humbled by the continuing resistance of parents and siblings to injustice and devaluation despite their own personal exhaustion and persistent systemic failures to actualize ostensible legal equality. We have had the particular privilege of working and sharing life, fears, tears,

---

[1] Among the myriad reasons that labels of disability are contentious is that labels objectify people. In an attempt to mitigate the dehumanizing effect of disability labels, some disability advocacy groups popularized person-first language that has prevailed primarily in the United States. Placing people before the disability is meant to focus on shared humanity, adding disability as simply one facet of the person. In the United Kingdom, the term "disabled people" is preferred, in that it focuses on the societal devaluing of the individual who diverges from the prescribed norm of corporeality. Michael Oliver, an originator of the social model of disability, argues that the person-first rationale "flies in the face of reality as it is experienced by disabled people themselves who argue that far from being an appendage, disability is an essential part of the self. In this view it is nonsensical to talk about the person and the disability separately and consequently disabled people are demanding acceptance as they are, as disabled people" (1990, xiii). Recognizing that any label is problematic, we choose to use both terms, in this way acknowledging the misconceptions and stereotyping that plague our social reception of what we view as human vulnerability and impairment.

and laughter with individuals and disability advocacy groups in Toronto, the Niagara Region, and Saskatchewan. We cannot begin to name everyone, but we are deeply grateful to every person for the beauty and sanctuary they create in this world. We are no less grateful to the disability rights movement and scholars in Disability Studies who have revealed the crippling effects of a medicalized perspective of disability and the power of "normalcy" on culture and society.

This book has been a collaboration of two primary areas of reflection: theology for Myroslaw and Disability Studies for Maria. Ideally, theory and practice are not separated when we believe what we teach. We have learned this first hand from the late Elizabeth Wilson, who taught us so much more than Latin and Greek by her generosity and love. To know her was to understand that being an icon of Christ was not a figurative concept.

Articulating one's belief inevitably leads to personal reflections of origin that must acknowledge parents and family. We both grew up in the experience of hospitality: visitors to our childhood homes could expect food, warmth, and a place to sleep, no matter what. Profound thanks to our parents for teaching us the heritage of our faith and culture and for maintaining our traditions in an environment which was, at that time, often alienating and unsupportive of "ethnicity." We are especially blessed in the legacy of Sophia, Maria's mother, who enfolded all people into the warmth of her kitchen. Differences made no difference when eating at her table.

In the various moves we have made with our own family, we have met beautiful friends, some of whom become family in our hearts. Among these we thank Patty and John Thompson, who have stayed with us in spirit even though we live thousands of kilometres apart. Thanks to you for reading the manuscript in the midst of your hectic schedules and thanks for always believing in us.

We want to acknowledge all the wonderful women who have assisted our daughter Aleksandra throughout the years, especially our friends Sarah and Sumera, without whom we would not have been able to write in many daytime hours.

Finally, we express our gratitude to our three daughters, Myroslava, Anastasia, and Aleksandra, who continue to teach us about life and love.

Why We Wrote This Book

My father died when I was ten. In retrospect, I recognize this life-changing event as the moment when I consciously confronted Christian piety and found it not only wanting, but downright insulting. I remember my visceral resistance, which at times amounted to hostility, to the mantric assurances that were showered on my family after my father's death. From childhood, I developed a certain scorn for the contradictory and ostensibly comforting platitudes that surround popular Christian discourse. It seemed that God, like the Olympian gods of antiquity, wrought havoc in people's lives and at times might miraculously remedy some situations on a whim, or in response to fervent pleading. Nevertheless, my mother brought us up with an unwavering faithfulness to our Byzantine Catholic tradition. In time I came to see a need to distinguish between our faith tradition and popular piety, but my ambivalence to Church and its take on life's vicissitudes grew.

Ironically, my husband became a Ukrainian Catholic priest. Over the 30 years of our life together, we have grappled with the dilemma of miracles and grief. After years of listening and sharing with others, we have finally arrived at the opportunity to marry our academic backgrounds of theology and disability studies in the humanities to write down our thoughts about living in the world as Christians. We focus on disability and our Christian tradition because we have learned that disability is an enduring, fundamental aspect of humanity that has been manipulated and wronged by society. We cannot strive to imitate Christ without acknowledging the intrinsic role of human disability with us and in us. We searched our faith tradition for signs of disability and, indeed, we found the Divine Trinity.

Maria Truchan-Tataryn

Introduction

You've won the jackpot! Is it for real? You stare at the notification and realize that the yelp of delight you heard just jumped out of your own mouth. This isn't the lottery, but an invitation to travel (all expenses paid) to Costa Rica. Your name has been chosen to represent your church community at an international conference of Christian lay ministry. You have been waiting for a reason to use the extra vacation days you have accumulated at work; everything is turning out perfectly!

A month later, you've arrived. As the shuttle delivers you to the conference centre, you thrill with the beauty of the environment and anticipation of the event. Elated, registration in hand, you follow the arrows to the designated ballroom for the opening reception. Groups of individuals chat and sip drinks; some are already engaged in animated discussions. As you make your way into the room, you hear various languages, spot interpreters, and ensure that your name tag with its Canadian flag is in full view. Hoping to be swept into a conversation as you approach the refreshments table, you notice that the attendants distributing the drinks do not see you. As you try to catch their eye, you realize that not only the servers, but also the other participants, are moving away slightly as you approach. Everyone is deliberately avoiding eye contact. Wait. Not everyone. A cluster of people farther off is staring—at you. As you draw nearer to them, they quickly turn their heads and move away. You check your clothes. Is something undone? What about your hair? Have you missed some protocol, some procedure? You know you have prepared carefully and thoroughly for this conference. You have an invitation. What is happening?

Finally, a concerned-looking woman approaches with the air of some-one in charge. "There you are!" she exclaims with strained and exaggerated good nature. "How nice that you've come! Oh dear, we were going to have a place for you. Don't worry, we will sort it out. Why don't you just wait out in the hall until I come back?" she twitters as she takes hold of your arm and steers you out of the reception room. In the ensuing blur, you feel all eyes focus on you. Someone says, "Isn't there a special place for ...?" Meanwhile, you have not had a chance to say a single word ...

Before you read this book, we hope you can imagine yourself in the above situation. Have you slugged the patronizing "rescuer" or given in to tears? What do you feel? Dismay? Disbelief? Anger? Self-doubt? Outrage? Disappointment? Humiliation? All of the above? More? We can all relate to the pain of rejection from our own specific experiences. Of course, every-one who applies for a job, auditions for a play, or tries out for a team cannot always be chosen. Accepting this type of disappointment and continuing to try again is regarded as standard development in a person's life. Some of us might remember the classic high school shunning of the "uncool," those with the misfortune to wear the clothes or live in the neighbourhood that flouted the mandatory fashion decreed by the arbiters of coolness. Buy the "right" jeans; take another bus route; conform. When you don't make the team or get the job, you can practise or improve your skills and then try again. But if you have been left out for being Asian, or female, for example, which brand of jeans will buy your membership? When you are not welcome simply for being as you are, for looking as you do (regardless of personality), you have no recourse. As with the opening scene above, you have no agency. Your exclusion is impersonal. Your being is unwanted even while your being has nothing to do with it. This curious, illogical predicament is, in essence, prejudice.

In our opening scene, you responded to an invitation to attend a desir-able event. You had a right to be there. From the nature of the conference, we can presume that all the participants, like you, were good citizens actively engaged in their church communities. People came from diverse regions around the world—all strangers to each other. What kind of recep-tion would you have expected? Why?

Our imaginary experience of rejection mimics a mundane social response to individuals perceived to be somehow different from the status quo. Details constituting difference depend on contexts, but the wounding visceral effects of unwarranted exclusion (simulated above) are familiar. In this book, we would like to reflect on social responses to difference, particularly as manifested in Christian communities. We will focus on social perception of difference that lies beyond the anomalous individual's control—specifically, the difference we label as disability. In the initial scene, there is no reason why you should not be welcomed as an equal. As leaders of church communities, we would not intentionally exclude fellow members. Unlike eras past, parish communities have been sensitized and are welcoming of gender, class, and ethnicized diversity. However, as a Church we have attended less assiduously (religiously) to the inclusion of people whose bodies fail to conform to society's mandate of normalcy. Unconsciously, communities continue to leave members in the drafty hallway despite sending them the same invitation received by those enjoying the cocktails.

Why focus on disability in the Christian Church? Christians do have a tradition of caring for the sick and unfortunate. Various Christian women's and men's associations have raised funds for charities that tend to the needy. Jean Vanier, the world's foremost champion of people with disabilities, is a devout Catholic. Admittedly, given our own background, we begin with experiences springing from Catholic practice, but we recognize that this spotlight illuminates a broader Christian Church and practice. Certainly, most Christian communities share a millennium of common tradition, and in the Western world, despite myriad variations, Christian communities share a desire to live according to Christ's teaching. In short, we share the struggle to be Christian. When we consider our parish community, or what we know as "typical" parish congregations, can we see the participation of members with wheelchairs, white canes, canine supports, sign languages or the like? Perhaps we can. More probably, we do not expect the pastor to use Braille or the choirmaster to need an elevator to reach the choir loft. Why?

In our culture, we learn to imagine disability as a tragedy that strikes the unfortunate. Disability is never expected, and its appearance tends to provoke discomfort, dis-ease. The affected individual must bear the burden of "coping" so that others will not feel burdened. Communities heroically rally around an accident victim, but after the initial excitement, the grind of daily existence for all parties often means a person with a disability is soon left to the routines of charitable ministries. We take for granted that the victim of tragedy passes on into a capable, albeit mysterious, realm of public services where experts manage all the needs.

Why should Christians need to approach disability issues any differently from our society as a whole? Do not our taxes provide professional social services? Why should we defy social norms and cultural expertise? Why destabilize the good work of church communities by imposing the meaningful inclusion of disabled people? Why introduce discomfort?

The answer is alarmingly simple: Christ. Christ's example of living; Christ's acknowledgement—nay, embrace—of women, Samaritans, children, lepers, tax collectors, and the like. Jesus distresses his followers by relentlessly transgressing the rules of social stigma. It appears that Jesus persists in hanging out with anyone outside the mainstream. Jesus shifts our understanding of the "holy" by calling all people to himself, especially those whom others have rejected. The Christian community, early on, recognizes its role as a supportive community, a community of sanctuary from the pagan world. The Christian Church was seen as a place of sanctuary, where members could find protection from the brutalities of the outside world. As members of Christian churches today, can we do any less?

1

Disabling/Disabled Communities

I n the late 20th and early 21st centuries, the Christian community has endeavoured to reinvigorate its prophetic voice, speaking out on issues of social justice, human rights, and ecology. Official apologies for participation in the systemic abuse of the Aboriginal population in residential schools throughout Canada mark a humbling acknowledgement of some churches' complicity in the oppression of populations that the establishment configured as Other. Burgeoning social justice initiatives such as Kairos and Development and Peace witness to a trend of resistance to mainstream values as our churches begin to acknowledge the disparity between dominant norms and Christ's teaching. As Christians, we are learning to challenge prophetically and to re-vision our social values. However, in the fervent desire to live the Gospel in our current global reality, we nonetheless perpetuate an institutionalized discrimination against a significant segment of the human population—people labelled with disability.

Who are these people? Although in our society we are accustomed to imagine disabled people as visibly identifiable bearers of physical and mental defects, in fact, *disability* is a thoroughly fraught term signalling a plethora of slippery associations that are neither distinctly defined nor easily understood.[2] What we, as a collective, view as impaired depends a

---

2 In this book, the collective "we" and "our" society refer specifically to the Canadian mainstream: middle class, no longer predominantly white, but inheriting a dominant history

great deal on cultural norms, relationships, and values. For example, your dependence on a car for transportation or eyeglasses for reading is not considered a disability, whereas dependence on a wheelchair for transportation or Braille for reading brands you as disabled. Furthermore, this type of branding could not go unnoticed. A disability label itself, regardless of your skills and potential, could severely restrict your choices in life. Your opportunity for education, employment, travel, and social relationships may narrow significantly, not because of personal aptitude but because of social attitudes that interpret a person with a disability as a defective human being. Prejudice against people with disabilities is so deeply entrenched and taken for granted in our culture and society that this prejudice seems natural. As a result, routine discrimination becomes largely invisible. As the political theorist Iris Marion Young observes, oppression is the result of prejudice

> embedded in unquestioned norms, habits, and symbols ...
> [O]ppression refers to the vast and deep injustices that some groups suffer as a consequence of often unconscious assumptions and reactions of well-meaning people in ordinary interactions, media and cultural stereotypes, and structural features of bureaucratic hierarchies and market mechanisms—in short the normal processes of everyday life. (41)

The worldwide disability rights movement is raising its voice in opposition to the normalized degradation of disabled people. This movement reveals how physical and attitudinal structures in society privilege some bodies by disabling others, rejecting the latter from full civic participation. In Canada, as elsewhere in the Western world, people with disabilities are unconsciously devalued and treated with a double standard that is considered unacceptable for non-disabled people. Consider the simple example of public washrooms. A restaurant would be sanctioned on many levels if it provided a washroom for men only. Similarly, if the eatery banned women customers because of a lack of facilities for them, there would be legal repercussions.

One problem is that what we have come to recognize as disability—a tragic personal misfortune that requires cure, stoic overcoming, or death—

that privileges white, non-disabled males. Generalized references to Western tradition refer to the dominant Euro-centric culture of central/western Europe and North America.

is a fiction, socially fabricated within historical contexts to promote social and political agendas. The categorization of people labelled with disability as "those" people, as "special," as Other is something of an absurdity, because traits of disability have always been part of human experience. Even the use of *disabled* as a categorization of people is problematic, considering that the term represents a limitless set of potential human anomalies that would not necessarily render anything in common between those bearing the label. A Harvard law professor who is female and blind might not relate to a homeless man in Sudbury who uses a wheelchair. Yet both would be categorized as *disabled*. The privileged position of the professor may preclude any disadvantage from a lack of sight, whereas the Sudbury man's economic poverty might result in a lack of access to opportunities that would be perceived as his personal incapacity. Disability rights activists have observed that discrimination is the only thing that all people with disabilities have in common (Wendell, 31). Furthermore, to conceive of people with disabilities as Other is nonsensical, in that disability is a social identity that is open to everyone. Disability does not discriminate. We will all enter this social category, if not by a slip on the stairs, then simply by living long enough. Disability is, and always has been, a fact of human existence. While disability is a human constant, our reactions to disability are culturally and historically relative. The British sociologist Michael Oliver argues that the construction of disability as *ab*normality functions as a natural resource to be exploited by a nondisabled power establishment. Disability is a marker of common human diversity. Our society has constructed disability as deviance and has benefited economically from its systemic exclusion (97). In short, disability issues are not the putative concern of special interest groups or charity drives. Disability issues concern every human being because, when we probe the experience of disability in our society and culture, we uncover the tyrannical control of normalcy over our collective consciousness.[3] Ultimately, in probing the

---

3   Disability studies scholars such as Lennard Davis, Jenny Morris, and Rosemarie Garland Thomson demonstrate how the stigmatization of disability drives power mechanisms of capitalism by instilling anxiety in individuals about their ability to conform to acceptable standards of bodily norms. People acquire strict regimens of self-vigilance to ensure normalcy. The fear of appearing abnormal creates a "tyranny of normalcy" that compels consumerist practices that prey on the need to conform to a constructed sameness. This requisite sameness necessitates deliberate distancing from those whose bodies simply cannot conform, thereby affirming the non-disabled illusion of normalcy.

meaning of disability, we confront the challenge of who we are and what we want to be as human beings.

Despite a Christian tradition that stands with the poor and marginalized, our churches have been slow to champion the rights of those most rejected by arbiters of mainstream acceptability. Christian churches continue to reinforce social norms and practices that devalue and dehumanize people whose bodies cannot conform to arbitrary prescriptions of how a body should look or act. Despite Jean Vanier's L'Arche movement, established in France in 1964 and now found worldwide, our Christian communities continue to regard people with disabilities as objects of pity and recipients of charity.[4] Attention to disability has generally spawned segregated homes, segregated ministries, and segregated prayer services, rather than a rediscovery of our Christian tradition with a radical vision of the integrity and interdependence of every human life that challenges the double standards and segregation practices of mainstream society. In this book, we strive to defamiliarize dominant enculturated perspectives of disability in order to demonstrate that the inclusion of people with disabilities into the understanding and living of Christian community is imperative in response to the Christian call to justice.

We cannot pretend to fulfill Jesus' mandate to love our "neighbour" only in exclusive gated communities, as it were. As long as we sustain, individually and institutionally, the stigma with which mainstream society has shackled people with disabilities, Christians and Christian churches are themselves shackled. They cannot approach the transfiguring perception of Christ in every human being and the security that arises not only from realizing a common humanity, but also from belonging to the family of God. By perceiving and treating disabled people as Other, we accept societal taxonomies of gradated human value, thereby rejecting the fullness of humankind and limiting our spiritual growth, both personal and collective. The fourth-century Saint Athanasius of Alexandria (c. 296–373) taught that God became human so we could become like God (54:3). By

---

4 When Jean Vanier was a young philosophy professor, he was dismayed at the inhuman conditions he witnessed in an institution for people with developmental disabilities in France. He invited two men from the institution to live with him in a small house he named "L'Arche" (the Ark). Thus began his international movement of sharing community and enriching lives between people with and without labels of disability.

rejecting the vital voice and presence of disability from our dominant consciousness of normalcy and communities of faith, we inhibit our quest, denying our need to become more fully human.

Confronting the ignored issue of disability strikes at more than a correction of improper etiquette towards a marginalized category of people in our churches. Confronting entrenched collective attitudes towards disability strikes at the heart of attitudes towards difference—for the attitudes of fear and separation are at the foundation of hatred and violence towards others. In other words, if we deal with our unexamined bias towards people with disability, we will advance towards liberating our collective psyche from an overwhelming fear of human diversity, including our own uniqueness. Acknowledging and valuing the incommensurability of our differences will surely foster peace in social relations on multiple levels.

Leonard Desroches argues that as the Christian Church struggles with relentless global injustice, terrorism, and violence, we must examine the "most feared, and yet urgent, of mysteries: love of enemy" (xiii). We suggest that facing this Gospel imperative includes the need to explore the endemic fear of an enemy perceived to be among us and even within us. Before we can fully understand our fear of the difference encompassed in those identified as enemies of the state, we must confront our fear of the difference that exists inescapably within our human condition. In order to contend honestly with the strife that emanates from fearful identifications of *us* and *them*, we, as both individuals and collectives, must contend with our unconscious response towards the ideological spectre of disability. At the same time, we must address the consequent exclusion from expected considerations of social justice, human rights, and Christian fellowship of those among us labelled as disabled.

When we imagine issues of discrimination and injustice, most of us do not include ourselves as perpetrators. Most of us do not imagine participating in a community that intentionally denigrates or neglects people because of their disability. As Christians, we try to be "good" ethical citizens, but how many of us have actively opposed immigration laws that forbid entry for a family with a member who has a disability? Have we considered the reason for developments of earlier and more accurate prenatal testing? Have we actively worked towards inclusive classrooms so our children learn to grow with each other, regardless of abilities? Do we notice when our work environments—our homes, workplaces, playgrounds, restaurants—are not accessible for everyone? Have we worked to build the Kingdom by openly transgressing socially constructed norms, which deny the humanity of many?

Chances are, when we are faced with a situation involving a person with a visible disability, most of us would not turn away; we would respond in the best way we know, offering any assistance we are able to provide. But, as one pastor pointed out, "We don't have many disabled people coming here." He assured me that "they" do not want to attend a regular Mass because it makes them uncomfortable; they feel different and people stare. This priest felt he was responding charitably towards a group of people with disabilities by "allowing" them to meet once a month in his church hall. He interpreted their discomfort in the main community life as "natural," because they did not fit in.

In essence, his view blames the group for their differences and justifies their segregation by claiming it is self-imposed. What is the alternative? What if this church minister presumed that the parishioners with disabilities belonged alongside other parishioners? It would take effort to learn how to accommodate the particularities of the people who seem too different to blend in with the average. It requires creativity. It would certainly necessitate dialogue with each person who needed accommodation. It would compel relationship. It would create sanctuary. In fact, it would be a testament to the example that Jesus presents to his disciples, often to their dismay: speaking to, eating with, noticing, and addressing the very people he was expected to shun. Whether he speaks with a Samaritan woman, cures the daughter of a Canaanite woman, or simply eats with tax collectors, establishing respectful human relationships is at the core of who Jesus is and who the Father is (Jn. 14:7). The God who is revealed to us in Jesus Christ is the God of committed, vibrant, and thus demanding relationships—in fact, we are the benefactors of this God of relationships, because that God calls us to be in union (divinized) for all eternity.

Conceivably, if a person is made to feel wanted and needed within a group, if she or he is welcomed and accommodated, that person feels comfortable enough to want to participate in the group. If the established members become familiar with unconventional participants, compulsions to stare will dissipate. An expectation that all participants belong, rather than a presumption that all participants are similar, can create an impulse to recognize common ground. If this logic seems circular, it is, all the same, practical. Exposure itself facilitates familiarity and comfort. The organized removal of people with disabilities from quotidian public spaces has been a major factor in promoting the social stereotyping and fear of disability as markers of Otherness.

Our current culture has become so inured to the separation of dis/ability and the peripheralization of people with disabilities that we do not notice the injustice. It is like the joke about the store owner who is incensed by legislation forcing him to ramp the steep set of stairs at the entrance to his store. "Why should I spend money on a ramp? For 20 years, not one person in a wheelchair has ever bothered to shop in my store!" Out of sight, out of mind. It is instructive to reflect on the effort involved in creating a dichotomy between dis/abled and striving to erase the *dis* segment of the binary from the nondisabled sight. An estimated 15 percent of any population has visible disabilities (*World Report*, 27). The percentage climbs when people with mental illness and people whose disabilities are hidden are included. There is no one (definitive) definition of disability. Since disabling traits are relative to context, no human being is exempted. Disability affects every person in society, yet we are accustomed to assuming disability as *special*, beyond everyday existence. As the disability rights movement protested this social process of erasure, academic faculties in the humanities turned their attention to the role of disability within our socio-cultural systems. Disability studies research is revealing the centrality of disability to the ways we have historically constructed ideas of ourselves and our world. Scholars have found that although people with disabilities are not central to the imagination of the dominant norm, a constructed image of disability does, in fact, pervade our collective psyche.

In this book we will explore the integral presence of disability within the Christian faith tradition and the absence of disability in the central dynamics of current communities. The life work of Jesus focused on standing with anyone disabled by social forces or illness. Christianity has revolved around *caritas* and love for others, always in theory, if not always in practice. And yet, present-day Christian communities in the Western world reflect social practices of segregation more than Jesus' example of solidarity for all members of God's family. It is time to recognize the signs of the times; it is time to join with the social and civil rights movement of disability in order to more fully express our Christian commitment to ourselves and collectively to our world.[5] The disability rights movement has identified the standard naturalized perception of disability in Western culture today as framed within a medical model of disability, which has pathologized unconventional bodies and has individualized disability as a personal tragedy. Medicalization configures people with disabilities as "sick" or "in-valid." The invalid must leave normal living until she or he is cured. Although disabilities may involve illness, disabled people are not necessarily sick.

By contrast, the social model of disability locates disability within society rather than in an individual. While not denying the exigencies of specific bodies, the social model focuses on the innumerable ways that society constructs disabling environments for citizens whose bodies cannot conform to a prescribed norm. Even what we presume to identify objectively as impairment in a person may depend more on social factors than on anatomical facts; we may be judging rather than simply observing. For instance, the (demographic) history of the small New England island of Martha's Vineyard illuminates the notion of disability as a social construction. From the seventeenth to the early 20th century, the island's population had an unusually high incidence of hereditary deafness. In Martha's Vineyard, all citizens, as a matter of course, "spoke" sign language. Since everyone was taught to be bilingual from childhood, deafness did not prevent anyone from community participation. Deaf people were typically middle class, and in the nineteenth century tended to have a higher level of education and thus higher status. While in other places deafness justified isolation, exorcism, or even death, in Martha's Vineyard deafness was not a disability (Groce). The experience of this island community shows how

---

5   The disability rights movement currently appears to be the last resistance movement to institutionalized bias. Although bigotry involving race, gender, class, and sexual orientation is far from eradicated, it is nonetheless illegal in North America. Prejudice against disability dominates policies in medicine, education, immigration, and employment without social censure. Like South Africa's regime of apartheid, when whites worshipped in Christian churches without acknowledging the insult of their social structures to Christian values, perpetuating society's devaluation of disabled people within our faith communities makes a mockery of our Christian commitment to justice.

societies define impairment by legitimating practices that either privilege and accommodate or devalue and peripheralize certain human realities.

To free ourselves from enculturated bias against the human reality we label as disability, we must unlearn the familiar prejudices of the medical model of disability and recognize the oppressive role of our physical and attitudinal structures towards unconventional bodies. Mindsets that have been entrenched for generations are not easily acknowledged, much less shifted. Unlearning prejudice can happen only with deliberate, conscious attention and effort. The attempt to begin perceiving society's role in constructing the phenomenon of disability reveals a number of issues that resonate loudly with Christian faith and tradition. As we come to realize that society is accountable for a great deal of the burden experienced by people who are disabled, we also come to understand that the onus for change is on all of us.

Society is not an autonomous entity, but rather a complex network of relationships. The systemic disenfranchisement of people not only signals institutional injustice but also indicts us as individuals who comprise society and inform its structures. We are not only made by society; we make the society by which we make ourselves. In short, every citizen is responsible for creating a more just society by striving to engage in relationships of equality and respect. Ivan Illich identifies the failure of social institutions as the failure to create such authentic human relationships. For Illich, sin is not a transgression of rules or laws, but a betrayal of relationship (62). This conviction echoes Jesus' (ultimately dangerous) habit of angering authorities by meaningfully engaging with others, regardless of ritual rules and caste. In this light, we as citizens have violated the rights of people with disabilities. Quite simply, we have sinned profoundly against disabled people. Our churches are equally indicted for reinforcing social norms based on instrumental values rather than the norm of inclusion (based on love) illustrated in Christ. However, as Christians we can refocus our communities on Christ's mandate of openness to each other and thereby nurture the growth of a society that values the wonder of human diversity and variability. Our faith tradition provides an inclusive understanding of humanity that can help defamiliarize our learned unconscious biases towards disability and liberate our fear of our own difference.

Reviewing our Christian heritage through a lens of disability lends astonishing clarity to the Gospel message of love: love for God, for neighbour, for self. This lens does not simply shed light on the failure of us as Church to mirror Jesus' example of forming communities. More acutely, this re-membering of our faith tradition provides exciting insight and joyful hope to our human condition, individually and collectively. Through Christ we are reminded of our human bodies and how our very embodiment—with its leakiness, limitations, beauty, and capability—participates in the living Trinity. Again recalling Athanasius, we remember that in encountering our humanness, we encounter God. We are enveloped by the Trinity.

Our third daughter, Aleksandra, was born in 1988; it was a normal pregnancy followed by a normal birth. Everything was fine for almost two years: feeding, walking, words. Then things began to go wrong: withdrawal, loss of skills, increasingly long periods of agonized scream-ing, no sleep. After a terrifying year, we received a tentative diagnosis: Rett Syndrome. Our pediatrician was devastated: "I can't think of a worse diagnosis" were her unforgettable words. She came to our home in the midst of a rainstorm to tell us herself. At that time the prognosis was mind-numbing: loss of all skills, withdrawal, our daughter locked in her body. Soon we were confronting another meaning of her diag-nosis. The queries from strangers, family members, and friends came as relentless assaults, accusations: "Can't they do something?" "Can't you put her somewhere?" "Can't you see this will destroy your family?" "Can't the doctors put her out of her misery?" While a few in our parish were extremely supportive, many seemed affronted. The social service network was there for people in her situation, right? We discovered that she might benefit from various physical therapies, but were told, "Sorry, with limited resources we only work with children who have a positive prognosis ...." Social services was hardly the panacea it purported to be on paper. We quickly learned that disability is our modern form of shun-ning. Our family was disabled by our community and our social system for failing to pass as normal and for causing disturbing ripples in the average calm. The collective response to Aleksandra's being uncovered a startling world we had never before encountered.

2

God—The Inclusive Community: The Trinitarian Paradigm

Perceiving disability through a social model rather than through the medical paradigm that has dominated the Western psyche for generations now is an essential step towards recognizing our bodily variations and limitations as an integral aspect of our humanity. In this book we are recovering a framework that responds to the human phenomenon of disability: the Trinitarian paradigm. This theological paradigm, rooted in our Christian heritage, is not intended to replace the social model, which has uncovered the disabling nature of our society for individuals who cannot conform to conventions of normalcy. However, the Trinitarian paradigm emphasizes the vital, universal need for human relationship. It illuminates and grounds human interdependence and values the human condition of incompleteness and capacity for connectedness.

The Trinity encapsulates Athanasius's instruction on the need to embrace our humanity in order to approach Divinity. An experience of disability heightens awareness of our corporeality and mortality, and debunks modern myths of individual autonomy, control, and human perfectibility. We cannot approach the fullness of humanity—and, consequently, our relationship with God—without embracing the integrally human condition of disability. Through the Incarnation, God became a person, sanctifying the human condition. Christ's humanity, therefore, calls us to a Trinitarian existence; a self-realization that continually reaches beyond individual selfhood to Otherness. In this book, we will reflect on the vital connection between Trinity and disability and how the notion of the Trinity, a God who is a community of being, means inclusive community. We will draw on the Eastern Christian theology of Iconography to reimagine dominant conceptions of the human body and to evoke an understanding of ourselves as Trinitarian beings.

Before approaching this Trinitarian theology of disability at the end of this book, we will examine some historical reasons for the deeply ensconced prejudices against disability that persist today, despite our national human rights legislation and democratic values. We will revisit Scriptural tradition (in Chapters 3 and 4) in order to see how the Gospel in the early Church (in Chapter 7) presents an inclusive and egalitarian model for human community. When we hear the prophetic call to justice, we can recognize our own compliance in the disabling of the Body of Christ by ignoring Jesus' example of openness to those denigrated and dismissed by socio-cultural standards. Before we can accept the Gospel challenge to actualize inclusive justice, we must first recognize how we contribute to the devaluation of people with disabilities. By examining the conflicting attitudes towards disabled people within Christian history and illustrating how they have been objects of social and religious oppression, we hope to highlight the limitations of our current ideologies of human culture, which largely reduce human worth to economic expediency.

In addition to a Scriptural review, in Chapter 6, we will reflect on the Patristic teachings (the teachings of the Church Fathers), with a focus on the fourth-century theological debates that crystallized doctrine concerning the nature of God and humanity. In that section we will try to dislodge the conditioned practice of projecting present-day bias onto interpretations of past events. We will consider the teachings of Athanasius, John Chrysostom (c. 347–407), and Maximus the Confessor (c. 580–662) on what it means to be human. In our historical review, we will discuss miracles and punishment, and we will demonstrate the difference between *caritas* and charity and their role in an ecclesial sense of justice. Listening to the voices of the disability rights movement enables us to be sensitive to and recover Gospel values more richly by understanding that equality does not entail sameness, difference does not entail deviance, and normalcy is not a natural phenomenon. Recovering our Christian heritage through a conscientization of disability liberates thinking from binary strictures, destabilizing canons of *us* and *them*, and facilitating a transformative and sacramental theology. Such a retrieval nurtures human community that grows from the acknowledgement of the fundamental dignity and inter-dependence of all human individuals.

We contend that *caritas* and justice are core elements of our Christian mandate that require assertive and transformative action. Living Gospel justice demonstrates that we share a common humanity and equal worth in the gaze of God. When living Gospel justice, we engage intentionally in relationship, especially in the spaces marked "impure" by the mainstream. Living Gospel justice deliberately creates communities of equals, thereby creating Trinity.

For many years, we were in a parish of mainly seniors. Our children were the only "young" people to be seen. Yes, it took these seniors time to get used to the chatter, the crying, and even the screaming, but they did. Our children loved the parish because they were enveloped by love and respect. It made no difference to our parishioners that our daughters were altar servers and that one had trouble walking. They accepted the fact that our youngest was unable to sit or stand still, that she would scream unexpectedly, and that our life was simply not going to conform to expected standards. But it was not just us they accepted. As more young people became church members, with all their (to be expected) attitudes and challenges, they, too, were accepted and respected. We all learned that community is messy, has many rough edges, and is where we get to know our God.

3

Deviating Bodies—Divine or Demonic: Our Hebrew Scriptural Tradition

The Law

More often than not, Christian church communities, especially in middle-class neighbourhoods, look fairly homogenous. It's not unusual for neighbourhoods to reflect a homogenous class or ethnicity. We find comfort in sameness. Ironically, the sameness we crave is a socially learned behaviour. Human beings share a fundamental humanity that is composed of endless variety.

Among many things, we share individual human uniqueness. The differences that separate us as people arise from contexts that teach us which differences to acknowledge and which to ignore. Our historical socio-cultural contexts teach us to categorize our common humanity into sameness and difference. For example, for generations, the notion of race has been considered an objective qualifier of people. However, "DNA analysis tells us that there is more genetic variation within a group we have called a race than within the entire human gene pool" (Davis, 14). Ultimately, we create sameness by targeting given human attributes as unacceptable and categorizing the remaining group of traits as the same (or at least not different). People with disabilities have been relegated to this status of unacceptable difference. But as we have pointed out earlier, disability is a very "normal" part of the human condition. Institutionalized attempts to erase the actual presence of disability from the consciousness and perspective of ordinary life experience have damaged not only people with disabilities, but also our collective humanity, compelling us to fear and hide our anomalies. Our comfortable middle-class church groups often do not include the percentage of people with disabilities that would be expected in any demographic. Why? Because the strongest barriers to the inclusion of disabled people are not physical. Ramps may facilitate entry of wheelchairs into a building, but the prejudicial attitudes against disability of those who enter by the stairs are often the hardest things to dismantle.

In Western culture, we are so accustomed to equating disability with tragedy and suffering that it takes some effort to get our heads around the notion of disability as simply a way of being. Stigmatizing unconventional bodily variety as defect, rather than accommodating and honouring particular ways of being, can disable people as much as or more than an impairment. Before reflecting further, we must acknowledge how problematic language becomes when discussing issues of value, identity, and ideological constructions. Saying that society's biased environments, both physical and attitudinal, disable people with anomalous bodies is not to diminish the very real hardships some people must endure because of disabling conditions. However, if an individual is treated with dignity and her community demonstrates that she is wanted, valued, and needed by ensuring that she is accommodated, her life will be rewarding.

Also, it is important to recognize the dilemma of generalizing about people with disabilities. We have pointed out that the single common trait linking people in this category is the discriminatory stigma attached to the disability label. Being a person with a disability means you are a person whom society putatively wants to eradicate, through prosthesis, abortion, segregation, sterilization, or divine miracle. This means disabled people must overcome, mask, hide, or prostheticize those parts of themselves that seem to offend the non-disabled mainstream.[6]

---

6   This mainstream devaluation pre-empts the possibility of seeing a "disabled" embodiment as desirable and satisfying, despite contrary evidence.

Society's attitudes frequently imply that unless you can function in a way that does not draw attention to your unconventional self, you have no right to "be." Human rights, civil rights, and equal rights do not easily adhere to someone whose humanity is attenuated, unconsciously, by dominant norms. If we revelled in our diversity as human beings, some conditions perceived as disabling would merely constitute a fresh stance for seeing the world, enriching the meaning of our humanity. Someone with a visual impairment may teach those with 20/20 vision another dimension to "seeing" the world. A person who is totally dependent on others for all aspects of care may be honoured for providing the opportunity to generate connection, compassion, and love among those around her. In essence, understanding disability as human diversity facilitates meaningful community as we reach out to each other and discover ourselves more deeply.

As Christians, we have a rich biblical tradition that illuminates the diversity of the natural world as reflecting God's creative energy. Recognizing the crucial state of creation as pluralistic, various, and multifarious facilitates rereadings of disability in sacred texts through a lens that is less coloured by current negative bias against disability. Our rereading of biblical portrayals of disability as diversity points to the need for further studies that will contextualize these images and explore their potential for expanded meaning.

Portrayals of illness, physical anomaly, and impairment permeate the Jewish and Christian Scriptural tradition. These images of disability arise from the fundamental theme of the Scriptures: humanity's relationship with God. Ultimately, the Christian Scripture illustrates the divine will for us, as human beings, to participate in that relationship fully and eternally. However, Scriptural accounts often convey conflicting perspectives on disability. At times, disability may seem to signal divine retribution, while at other times, people with disabilities are represented as bearers of divine grace. In order to arrive at a contemporary theology of disability, we must look more closely at the Christian salvation story.

Creation

Salvation history is rooted in the Hebrew Scriptures, which begin at the beginning, responding to the puzzling matter of origin. Where do we come from? Although Christian salvation history is at times conceived as a response to an odious mistake—original sin—it is above all a statement about a God so gracious that God desires to create.[7] This theme of creation rendered by grace is reinforced in the specific Christian story, where the Resurrection of Jesus is understood as re-creation and the day of Resurrection as the eighth day of creation. Salvation, then, is about a relationship initiated and sustained by God. It is about an unequal partnership between the all-powerful divinity and a limited creation. Salvation history does not present a story of similitude, but of irreducible difference. Yet, significantly, this difference is the prerequisite to community.

The Genesis accounts of creation profile diversity persistently from beginning to end, although this detail has often been overlooked.[8] Genesis 1:2 describes God transforming "a formless void" into different spaces such as light (1:3), day and night (1:5), and separate waters (1:6). In the two accounts of the creation of humanity, difference is also central. In the first account (Gen. 1:1–2:3), God creates "humankind" as a plurality, where difference is fundamental: "male and female he created them" (1:27). Humans are neither wholly attached to the created order nor completely identical to the divine; they are created, but in the image and likeness of the divine. They are not destined for unchangeable constancy, but are instructed to "Be fruitful and multiply" (1:28). They are to manage the differences that have been created: the fish, the birds, every living thing. The summary reflection upon this panoply of diversity is that "God saw everything that he had made, and indeed, it was very good" (1:31).

The second creation account (Gen. 2:18-25) similarly speaks of God as the creator of diversity: earth and heaven, plants and herbs, ground and waters. In fact, the lack of diversity—having created just a man—leads God

---

7   We will keep with the tradition that refrains from using specific gendered pronouns for God, recognizing that assigning gender to God limits our understanding of the Holy Trinity as being immeasurably beyond our human categories, especially those that reflect temporality and physicality, as do gender designators.

8   There is more than one story of creation in the book of Genesis. Biblical scholarship has helped us recognize that the Pentateuch (first five biblical books) is comprised of volumes that were compiled from various oral and perhaps written traditions and then edited into one volume. As a result, for example, we have a story of creation wherein "man" is created first (Gen. 2:4f.) and then "woman," and another story where both male and female are created simultaneously (Gen. 1:1–2:3). Further, the Flood story (Gen. 6:5f.) is regarded as a Hebrew retelling of common Middle Eastern creation stories.

to reconsider his actions and recognize that difference is important: "It is not good that man should be alone" (2:18a). Thus the creation of difference and relationships is an improvement on what could have been a moribund status quo. In this account, "man" immediately is given the task of naming the creatures God had created. This act of naming symbolically indicates that "man" is responsible for the ordering of creation. Yet the very act of ordering creates a further need: "but for the man there was not found a helper as his partner" (2:20). By ordering, that which has been created "man" has created a hierarchy, which produces in "man" a further need: a relationship of equality, a "partner." This need in the narrative gives rise to the creation of "woman." Human community is based in the difference between "man" and "woman." Difference is the very foundation of relationship and does not need to be overcome in order to create community. Human difference, as reflected in Scripture from the very point of origin, gives rise to community.

A third account of creation, or re-creation, is found in the story of Noah (6:5–8:19). Here we find the divine conundrum: human community has turned in on itself: "the earth was filled with violence" (6:11), and so the Creator must act to "correct" creation's fault. One could presume that the source of this violence was the very diversity that had arisen from the original divine command to multiply: difference could have fed hostility and misunderstanding. However, the text has subtly introduced another cause for concern: the breaching of the divine-human boundary (6:18). This fundamental difference between humans and God must be maintained, or else the primordial order is disrupted. Misunderstanding the nature of difference and diversity is more problematic than diversity itself. Thus, Noah, in being saved, is instructed to preserve diversity: "you shall come into the ark, you, your sons, your wife, and your sons' wives with you. And of every living thing, of all flesh, you shall bring two of every kind into the ark" (6:18-19). The covenant God establishes with Noah is based in the diversity of creation and echoes the divine words in Genesis 1:28: "be fruitful and multiply" (8:17 and 9:1, 7). This covenant is established not only with humanity, but also with "every living creature" (9:10). Significantly, the sign of the covenant is the rainbow (9:13), with its colours symbolically reflecting the diversity of creation.

Within the creation episodes we find critical faith-filled reflections on core aspects of the human condition: sin and human pluralism. The biblical story of the Fall in Genesis 3 presents human diversity deriving from God's compassion for the solitude of Adam. However, sin is born when Adam betrays God's trust: "Have you eaten from the tree of which I commanded you not to eat?" (3:11). The sin of Adam alters the nature of human diversity. The two individuals become adversaries, refusing to take responsibility for their actions. Adam blames Eve and Eve blames the serpent. Human childbirth—the fruit of the most intimate act of male–female interrelatedness—shall be painful; the ground upon which Adam walks shall be "cursed." Adam and Eve shall no longer look upon each other with openness and joy, but rather, in their post-Fall state, they "knew that they were naked" (3:7) and desired to cover themselves before each other's eyes.

Sin distorts Adam and Eve's perception of the divinely created and blessed plurality of their beings. Seen through the lens of sin, the diversity that reflects human giftedness from God becomes a cause for antagonism, distrust, pain, and betrayal. In this way, the story following Genesis becomes a story of betrayal and fraternal enmity. Cain, resenting the Lord's attention towards his brother, Abel, ignores the warning that "If you do well, will you not be accepted? And if you do not do well, sin is lurking at the door; its desire is for you, but you must master it" (4:7). Cain doubly breaks the bond of human relatedness by killing Abel and by abnegating his inherent responsibility for his brother: "Am I my brother's keeper?" (4:9). The brothers' story demonstrates the power of sin—not only to contravene the divine–human relationship, but also to fundamentally distort human relationship.

The Tower of Babel

Another story of human origins where sin, divine action, and human diversity converge is the story of the Tower of Babel. This narrative, rooted in Babylonian history, grapples with the meaning of Babylonian towers, or ziggurats, and language diversity. Yet again, sin and diversity are interrelated. The dwellers of Babel choose to build a tower "with its top in the heavens" as an expression of their own egos ("so make a name for ourselves") (Gen. 11:4). They do not value their unity and community for anything other than its potential to express their power or dominance. Because "nothing that they propose to do will now be impossible for them" (11:6), the Lord steps in. Human diversity generates from the divine intention to teach humanity of the need to reach beyond individual ego towards relationship with God and with each other. "The Lord confused the language of all the earth; and from there the Lord scattered them abroad over the face of all the earth" (11:9). Once again, human diversity and human interdependence are depicted as divinely intended realities within our human condition. Sin acts as a barrier blocking our ability to understand this gift.

Leviticus

Yet if diversity and interdependence are divinely inspired, what of frailty, illness, and disability?[9] Are there grounds for pious sentiments that portray disability as a deliberate act of God, either as a piece of a mysterious divine puzzle (God's choice) or as penalty for sin (God's judgment)? This question especially arises when reading the book of Leviticus and its myriad prescriptions concerning purity and impurity. In Leviticus 12, the woman who gives birth is unclean for a specific time, as is a woman during her menstrual period (2–5), a person with leprosy (13:3), and any man [who] has a discharge "from his private parts" (15:2). Uncleanness is delineated throughout the text. How does one interpret these codes in light of our previous reflection on diversity as divine will, especially when a person with a disability or mental illness is considered unclean?

---

9   Although it is problematic to suggest that disability is conflated with debility, for our purposes these categories constitute a population marginalized because of the state of their bodies. The conflation of disability with illness and weakness is one of the ways that deeply entrenched cultural attitudes stereotype and oppress people with disabilities. The modern medicalization of disability has further naturalized a prejudice that presumes that the presence of an identified impairment necessarily includes frailty, illness, and pain. Although these factors may accompany a disability, they do not exclusively feature in the life of a disabled person any more than they do in a non-disabled person's life. The conflation of disability with weakness and suffering contributes to the reasons why non-disabled people fear and avoid association with those who are labelled with disability. A fear of illness and pain translates into a fear of those presumed to be ill and in pain. However, consider how one who works as a delivery person needs a car for employment, but is not considered weak without one. On the other hand, it is common for a person using a wheelchair for mobility to be overlooked for employment she or he is qualified for because she or he is considered frail and a liability.

First, and perhaps most significantly, contemporary scholarship reveals that the law codes of Leviticus do not come from the time of Moses. Rather, their claim to be instructions of the Lord to Moses and Aaron are the attempt of a later editor to heighten their authority by associating them with the Exodus story and Moses' revelation on Sinai. These Levitical Codes, and all of what is termed the Priestly tradition, originate from the time of the Babylonian Exile (around the sixth century BCE). This Priestly tradition constitutes much of the Pentateuch, and includes not only Leviticus, but also parts of Genesis, Exodus, and Numbers. These texts, which were recorded by the Jerusalem Temple priesthood, document not only their insights, but also their reception of the priestly lore of their community. The goal of these texts was to preserve, in the midst of the Exile, the entire history of Israel from creation to its establishment in the Promised Land. They also wished to secure in the consciousness of their readers a normative authority for practices and traditions that had become part of Israelite culture and for which they, as the priests, had assumed a certain power of control.

The codes in Leviticus are not about the nature of humanity, but rather the character of Israel as a newly constituted worshipping community. "Israel is conceived as a 'congregation' ('edah) or religious community which not only witnesses to Yahweh's redemptive act of the Exodus but articulates the creation's praise of the Creator" (Anderson, 425). Leviticus's purpose is order, ritual, and the authority of the priestly caste, not complicated by human diversity. The self-interest of the Levitical texts is to validate the norms that can distinguish Israel as the Lord's true worshipping community. As Disability Studies scholars demonstrate, historically, the deliberate construction of normalcy relies on a concurrent delineation of abnormalcy. The priestly tradition established norms for those who were within the holy community by relegating some to the margins of that community, or excluding them entirely.

Thus, in Leviticus, the many prohibitions relating to people with disabilities arise within the context of defining what constitutes full participation in the worshipping community. The French historian Henri-Jacques Stiker reads Leviticus as declaring disabled people unclean and therefore unable to function as priests of the Temple (24). However, others, particularly scholars of the Hebrew Bible, offer a more nuanced perspective. Judith

Abrams distinguishes between physical—that is, visible—disabilities and others that are not easily observed.

> The priest, as we have already seen, mediates between heaven and earth, between holy and profane. To survive in such a dangerous position, the priest had to be fit for the company of angels: blemishless, pure of lineage, and untouched by the taint of death (i.e., ritually pure) … Deafness, mental illness, and mental disability are not mentioned in this passage, perhaps because they were not considered readily visible defects. (23)

Abrams contrasts this desire for bodies unmarked by anomaly to the later rabbinic approach that saw mental disabilities as most troublesome. Nonetheless, even when considering the prohibitions in Leviticus, Abrams draws attention to further nuances. She contends that once in the priestly line, whether one functions as a priest or not, or whether one has a disability or not, that individual maintains his status as "priest." She notes,

> More serious problems for a priest would be a defect in lineage, which would utterly disqualify him not only from officiating at the cult but from receiving priestly emoluments, or a state of ritual impurity, which would deprive him of these same benefits. Thus a priest in a state of ritual impurity is more disabled than a priest who is blind: while a blind priest may still consume the food set aside for him, a priest who is ritually impure cannot. (26)

The origins of linking disability and ritual impurity are unclear; however, two common explanations emerge within the history of interpretations. First, and most commonly, physical perfection (however defined) is associated with the divine. Thus the priest, the mediator between heaven and earth, must approximate that perfection. Therefore, not only in Judaism but also in other religions, and very markedly in Roman Catholic Christianity, the notion of God-likeness or Christ-likeness in some particularly tangible and physical ways (celibacy) is attached prescriptively to the priesthood. In Leviticus, a perceived physical defect, or, more accurately, a physical characteristic excluded by the community's constructed notion of perfection, means one cannot fully function as priest.

Another explanation is rooted in third- to seventh-century Judaic commentaries that regard disability as "linked here with vulnerability to moral shortcomings" (Abrams, 69). However, this is not the case because disability is a penalty for immorality, but because it represents an "undefined moral state," a danger to the community because of its uncertainty. Abrams notes the difficulty society had in "placing" those marked by disability into its ordered self-understanding. She argues that "the disqualification of persons with disabilities from this ritual could be a blessing or a curse" (69). Nevertheless, an indistinctly defined state challenges interpretation; it provides the possibility of either acceptance or rejection. Ultimately, disability is interpreted negatively; what is interpreted as physical defect is seen as embodying moral defect. Israel's "immorality is symbolized by various physical disabilities" (Abrams, 76). Once more, the priestly intent to demarcate an unquestionable obligatory morality meant that a lack of clarity, not necessarily explicit immorality, threatened the ostensibly immutable moral state of the community. Impurity was considered a pollution—not destroying purity, but obscuring and therefore jeopardizing it. Disability is not accepted as a commonplace phenomenon of the divine creation; disability is feared as an erosion of an originary state, threatening Israel's worthiness before the Lord as a faithful worshipping community.

From Levitical Impurity to Medieval Demons

This religious abhorrence of "deformity" has lingered within Christianity. Martin Luther (1483–1546) is often cited as an example of someone whose views were particularly condemnatory.[10] A famous passage from his *Table Talks* refers to a twelve-year-old boy, probably with an intellectual disability. Luther recommended that the boy be drowned, since "such changelings were merely a mass of flesh, a *massa carnis*, with no soul … The Devil sits in such changelings where their soul should have been" (Kanner, 7). In an age obsessed with monstrosity and miraculous cures, Luther was not exceptional, although in defending infant baptism he questions the value of reason as a prerequisite for faith. The preceding Middle Ages are known as a period when any form of mental abnormality was regarded as a sign of demonic possession; Luther explicitly regarded "all dangerous diseases" as "blows of the devil" (53).

---

10 For a more extensive discussion of Luther's views on disability, see M. Miles, "Martin Luther and Childhood Disability in 16th Century Germany: What Did He Write? What Did He Say?" *Journal of Religion, Disability, and Health* 5, #4 (2001): 5–36.

It is well known that persons with physical abnormalities were put on display and mocked in village fairs (Cusack, 417; Winzer, 91–95). Ambroise Paré (c. 1510–1590) developed a list of causes of monstrosity and deformity. First on the list was "resulting from God, intended for God's glory"; the second, "emanating from the wrath of God"; and the twelfth and last, "being changelings of the devil" (Yong, 36). Even the Enlightenment philosopher John Locke (1632–1704) regarded those with "mental or rational defects" as not human and, when recognized in infancy, justifiably killed (Yong, 37). Since they were not human, they lacked the potential for eternal life and so their elimination was necessary "so as not to give room to the devil" (Yong, 37). The apparent prevalence of such manifestations of the "devilish" heightened the appeal of the miraculous.

We must acknowledge this trajectory of thought, since these horrific conclusions linking anomaly and Satan are so damaging and sensational that their persistence has at times eclipsed the Christian heritage of inclusion that has been consistently sustained, but with less fanfare. The denigration of those marked with deviance is a perversion of Christ's message and a glaring distortion of the faith tradition.

The Levitical devaluation of disabled bodies, however, is challenged and reinterpreted in other sections of the Hebrew Bible. In Genesis, despite the negative priestly attitudes towards physical disability, a limp signals God's favour in the story of Jacob (32:25-31). Jacob victoriously wrestles with a stranger, interpreted either as an angel or as God. Unable to defeat Jacob, the stranger strikes Jacob's hip, causing him to walk with a limp. Jacob marvels at his encounter with God: "I have seen God face to face, and yet my life is preserved" (32:30). In Canaan, God renames Jacob "Israel" (35:10), a name commonly understood as "the one who struggled with God" (Coote, passim). Thus, in salvation history, Jacob's disability is a sign of Jacob's newly found esteem before God.

Similarly, the greatest of the Hebrew leaders, Moses, describes himself as "slow of speech and slow of tongue" (Ex. 4:10), presuming that these characteristics would disqualify him from the position of leader of the Hebrews. In response, God claims responsibility for individual attributes ("Who gives speech to mortals? Who makes them mute or deaf, seeing or blind?" [4:11]) and affirms divine support: "I will be with your mouth and teach you what you are to speak" (4:12). Moses' ostensible speech "defect" becomes not a sign of disfavour but rather a vehicle for divine power. What the human Moses perceives as disabling is simply an occasion for the manifestation of divine engagement in human circumstance, reminding us that all human attributes are dependent upon God.

Liminality

The Jewish sages of the third to seventh centuries grapple with this notion of the ambiguity of disability. They regard physical disabilities as "the outcome of life processes" (Abrams, 122) and do not give them moral weight. Intellectual disabilities, on the other hand, are seen as potentially manifesting an inner disorder. Abrams argues that the sages' system placed disabled people in a liminal space.

> Like Turner's neophytes, people with disabilities were experienced as neither fully dead nor fully alive. Therefore, they are "structurally 'invisible' (though physically visible) and ritually polluting ..." They have no status, property, insignia, secular clothing, rank, kinship position, nothing to demarcate them structurally from their fellows. Their condition is indeed the very prototype of sacred poverty ... They are therefore betwixt and between full personhood and nonpersonhood. (128)

The liminality rendered by the ambiguous state of the disabled person illustrates how the interpretation of a non-disabled establishment imposes a constructed meaning onto a less powerful minority. Disability garners its negative stigma not from the specific attributes of individuals, but from the way society is structured to privilege some types of bodies or intellectual capacities while dismissing the personhood of others who cannot conform to the imposed norm. The poverty, devaluation, and alienation are socially imposed and enforced.

Current Disability Studies scholarship frequently evokes the notion of disability as liminality. In his groundbreaking work on society and disability in the United States, the anthropologist Robert Murphy describes the liminal status of disabled people as "ritually polluted" (133), signifying a type of death to former social status, imprisoned in the in-between, neither dead nor alive, but forbidden to re-emerge into the requisite wholeness of the mainstream. His experience echoes the liminal position conceived by the Jewish sages. In contrast, other scholars focus on liminality as the space of ritual transition between social identities. In Turner's study of initiation rites, the participant figuratively and often literally leaves the community to enter into an ambiguous space beyond the known order so as to reappear transformed. (For example, a boy child leaves his family home for a period of wilderness training with elders. He returns no longer a boy, but a man.)

This emphasis on the transitional and transformational process of liminality is salient on multiple levels from a Disability Studies perspective. Tanya Titchkosky argues that disability presents a "potentially radical space of between-ness" (237) where conventional values meet the personification of their resistance, offering "alternative ways of being-in-the world" (237). The very "lack" with which disability is stigmatized, Titchkosky concludes, lends it the ambiguity of liminality, "and this ambiguity ironically clarifies our understanding of the body and how it might speak to the human condition" (239). Similarly, Rosemarie Garland Thomson interprets disability's liminal situation as one of "pure possibility" (249).

Once the liminality of disability is acknowledged by mainstream society, the ambiguity of being human is illuminated. Because the re-entry of the liminal individual into society necessarily shifts the space entered, the transitional process invites social transformation with each emerging individual. In this way the incorporation of perspectives from discounted forms of embodiment promises to revitalize all perception, defamiliarizing habitualized practice and bringing it into renewed being. The liminal space delineated by disability scholars entails an ongoing process of emergence for the person with a disability, not as an assimilated sameness or tolerated difference, but rather as a transformer, a valued member of a society who draws on "incoming" perspectives for meaning. While suffering the disenfranchisement of a stigmatized identity, a position of disability has the ironic potential benefit of a somewhat perverse freedom that reveals the limitations of normalcy (Thomson, 250). Perhaps the mainstream impulse to control and contain disability is less a fear of contamination than a fear of the ambiguity of power in "difference."

We believe that reading Scriptural tradition through the lens of a social model of disability draws us into such a liminal space of possibility, both deepening and expanding our consciousness of relationship with

God, humanity, and the created world. In our Trinitarian paradigm, this liminal space of possibility is the space of sanctuary—the Kingdom is already, but not yet. In this sanctuary, rooted in the life of the Trinity, we reject the established and constructed order of this world. Recognizing our being in the image of the Trinity, we are empowered to grow in actualizing a new vision and new life. In the fourth century, Gregory of Nyssa (c. 335–c. 394) articulated the dynamic vibrancy of this liminality: "Let us change in such a way that we may constantly evolve towards what is better, being transformed from glory to glory, and thus always improving and ever becoming more perfect by daily growth, and never arriving at any limit of perfection" (52).

The Prophets

At the heart of the Hebraic prophetic tradition is a two-fold message: God has acted in a loving and caring manner towards the people, and the appropriate response to that divine action is "faithfulness, to be expressed in prayerful worship and in righteous living. The latter included, in particular, special concern for the vulnerable members of the community" (Cook, 306). But the prophets distinguish between those who are vulnerable or weak and those who are faithless and suffer as a result. The latter is the result of sinfulness and so "the antidote for suffering is to repent of one's sins and live in faithfulness to the Lord" (Cook, 11). The vulnerable are the victims of oppression and inequality produced by societal evil, and "the vulnerable members of the community are entitled to special care by the group" (Cook, x). The lack of solicitude for members of the community is, for the prophet Amos, an affront to the special relationship of God and the people (Cook, 64). The prophet Micah proclaims "divine intervention on behalf of the lame, the banished and the wounded" (89, ref. Mic. 4:6); the promised result proclaimed in verse seven is that those God gathers will become a remnant and a powerful nation, with the Lord as their leader forever" (Cook, 89–90). Isaiah roundly condemns those who propagate social injustice: "Ah, you who make iniquitous decrees, who write oppressive statutes, to turn aside the needy from justice and to rob the poor of my people of their right" (Is. 10:1-2).

Those in need are recognized and supported by the Lord: "He gives power to the faint, and strengthens the powerless. Even youths will faint and be weary, and the young will fall exhausted; but those who wait for the Lord shall renew their strength, they shall mount up with wings like eagles, they shall run and not be weary, they shall walk and not faint" (40:29-31). Unlike the priestly attitude that judged corporeal impairment as a reason for rejection from the faithful community, in the prophetic writings God's presence embraces those in need. Correction of a perceived flaw is not mandated for inclusion in the community. Faith brings God's strength to individuals in any state of being. These poetic lines, taken out of context and read with the current prevalent prejudice against disability, may fuel expectations of miraculous cures that, when not forthcoming, become the source of blaming the victim whose faith is too weak. Nevertheless, the texts confirm God's embrace of every member of the community, particularly those who are seen to be in need.

In Jeremiah's pivotal sermon (Jer. 7:1-28), around which his whole ministry is structured, he reminds people that true worship does not lie solely in the offering of prayers or holocausts, but rather in repentance of deeds:

> If you truly act justly one with another, if you do not oppress the alien, the orphan, and the widow, or shed innocent blood in this place, and if you do not go after other gods to your own hurt, then I will dwell with you in this place, in the land that I gave of old to your ancestors for ever and ever. (7:5b-7)

The prophetic call to Israel is a call to be a community of justice. In the just community, God's graciousness resonates in the relations among all members. As God embraces the needy, so, too, communities of faith reach out to grant strength to every person in her or his specific state. In the just community, the less fortunate other—"alien," "orphan," "widow"—will not be oppressed by the daily social and cultural prejudices that erode one's dignity.

According to Jeremiah, God dwells with the faithful community that cares for all of its members. Similarly, Hosea calls Israel to demonstrate to all people the *hesed* (mercy) that God has shown them. A lack of fidelity, mercy, and knowledge of God (4:1) causes social disorder and, therefore, divine condemnation. Zechariah thus encapsulates the prophetic challenge: "Thus says the Lord of hosts: Render true judgements, show kindness and mercy to one another" (Zech. 7:9). This call is particularly relevant for those whom a society has judged to be peripheral, needy, weak, or disabled, since it is the entire community that is called to be sanctuary.

David

In 2 Samuel 4–19, a story from the life of King David exemplifies the creation of just community through faithfulness to personal and collective bonds of relationship between David and Meribbaal, who "was lame in both his feet" (2 Sam. 9:13).[11] Meribbaal is the grandson of King Saul, who betrays the covenant he held with the family of David. During the ensuing battle, the five-year-old Meribbaal falls from the arms of his fleeing nurse. Ostensibly, the unfaithfulness of the little boy's fathers (father and grandfather) results in their deaths and in the innocent Meribbaal's disablement when he suffers a literal "fall." However, any interpretation of this event as punishment is precluded by the story's portrayal of social responsibility and faithfulness to relationship. Once established as king, David seeks out the exiled Meribbaal in order to restore and honour the covenant between their families. David brings the "lame" Meribbaal into his kingdom as his equal, not as a subordinate; he offers Meribbaal a place at his table. "David said to him, 'Do not be afraid, for … I will restore to you all the land of your grandfather Saul, and you yourself shall eat at my table always.'" (9:7).

Immobility has not attenuated Meribbaal's well-being or sexuality. He has an infant son. Nor does Meribbaal's disability deter the King of Israel from adopting him into the royal family. Fully aware of the king's beneficence, Meribbaal repays him with loyalty: "For all my father's house were doomed to death before my lord the king; but you set your servant among those who eat at your table" (2 Sam. 19:28). The story's lesson is one of enduring mutual love and loyalty rather than strategic war alliances or personal dominance and power. Meribbaal is not expected to "earn" his place at the table. Although he is not self-sufficient and needs specific care and accommodation, Meribbaal is valued by King David; both are loyal to each other and to the covenant between their houses.

Their faithfulness, and specifically David's embrace of "lame" Meribbaal, is contrasted with the servant Ziba's exploitation of Meribbaal's disability for his own personal gain. Ziba betrays his role and position as

---

11 Meribbaal, which means "beloved of the Lord," is also translated as Mephibosheth, meaning "one who scatters shame" or "exterminator of idols."

a trusted family servant of three generations. He also betrays the personal relationship he has with his master, Meribbaal, by denying him essential aid and slandering him as a traitor. Ziba deliberately abandons Meribbaal in the city, refusing to help him onto his animal when David's followers are expected to follow him out of Jerusalem. When Ziba reports to David that Meribbaal has deceived the king and has joined the enemy, Ziba inherits all of his master's wealth. Ziba takes advantage of Meribbaal's vulnerability and profits from his ruin. Ultimately, David regains Jerusalem and discovers his friend's fidelity and love. In this story of the House of David, disability is featured as an ordinary human occurrence that does not interfere with relationships of faithfulness. Significantly, the deceitful, covetous figure abuses the disabled character, framing Meribbaal for the betrayal Ziba embodies.

A salient lesson from this brief review of the Law and the Prophets is that sacred history is written from a historical context. Because that context is currently unfamiliar to us, the texts are at risk of being misread. And yet, we see that disability persistently plays a role in these narratives that form the archives of our faith. As much as the Book of Leviticus seems to limit involvement of individuals with impairments of any kind, the prophetic writings highlight disability in the context of social justice, good relationships, and divine goodness. In the Gospels, Jesus is portrayed as a prophet as well as a fulfillment of the prophets with an unequivocal call to value all humanity in the Kingdom of God.

When people look at our daughter, Aleksandra, what do they see? Someone who can't talk, someone who drools, someone who does not believe in personal space and is literally in your face? Some see the sign of sin. We have been interrogated about our conduct: drugs, promiscuity … there must be a cause. Some search further back for familial guilt: For whose past actions is she atoning? Some see only a social burden, a cost, a nightmare for teachers. How many just see Aleksandra? How many just see a human being to be embraced, respected, loved? How difficult is it to see Christ in her? How difficult is it to be Christ with her?

4

The Radical Rabbi: Jesus Disables Normalcy

··

The Gospel accounts place Jesus of Nazareth squarely within the prophetic proclamation of justice and within the lineage of David. At the same time that Jesus embodies tradition, he also radicalizes his followers and shocks his contemporaries. In the Gospels, Jesus unequivocally embraces diversity and demonstrates a desire, a possibility, and a process of inclusion of the most marginalized sectors of society. Women, prostitutes, children, lepers, Romans, individuals with disabilities, demoniacs of different varieties, Samaritans, and tax collectors are among those whom Jesus approached personally, seeking relationship, affirming their dignity and inviting them into the Kingdom. "Jesus says explicitly that the sick, the disabled, the marginalized, are the first in the Kingdom of God" (Stiker, 34). Calls to enter into faith-filled relationships with individuals who have been largely rejected by the mainstream might produce more discomfort than helping to distribute meals to shut-ins. However, living Christian faith is as radical and destabilizing as God becoming human. Striving to become more deeply human by following the example of Jesus is uncomfortable, since there is no time for the comfort that leads to complacency. Christian love always reaches out to embrace the other, for "there is no other sacred than the relations to one's fellows" (Stiker, 35).

A Kingdom of Inclusion

The oldest Gospel, the Gospel of Mark, presents the first words of Jesus as being "The time is fulfilled, and the kingdom of God has come near" (Mk. 1:15). Standing in the prophetic tradition, Jesus proclaims the immanence of the Kingdom. This Kingdom, which is not of this world, burst onto the scene as a disruption of social expectations: "Blessed are the poor in spirit, for theirs is the kingdom of heaven. Blessed are those who mourn, for they will be comforted." (Mt. 5:3-4). The Beatitudes establish a Kingdom normalized not by exclusion and power, but by inclusion and service. The norm for action is not judgment or chastisement, but forgiveness and healing, because they build the sacred bond between God and humanity, and among people. Mark's Gospel persistently inscribes events where individuals who are disabled and marginalized by their community are enfolded by Jesus's caring attention, restoring them to community. After he calls the first disciples (Mk. 1:16-22), Jesus is portrayed as a healer, healing the demoniac (1:23-28), the mother-in-law of Simon Peter (1:29-31), a series of people who are ill and possessed (1:32-34), a leper (1:40-45), and a man paralyzed (2:1-12). Jesus' action is one of nullifying the established norms that have disrupted community. By approaching and engaging with individuals who have been rejected by the cultural and ritual codes of the community, Jesus subverts the taboos of exclusion and practises radical inclusion. In Jesus' order there is no longer a "leper" or a "woman" or any categorical determining of moral status. Instead, whomever Jesus confronts, he invites to be with him, to be with God.

By recognizing people's faith in the first instance, he demonstrates that God embraces those whom society marginalizes in the name of a self-serving holiness and thus that these people should be welcomed into the sanctuary of the sacred community. Stiker asserts that the actions of Jesus confuse previous distinctions between the sacred (pure) and profane (impure). "Only one thing is sacred, and that is human fellowship, which can be profaned by lack of respect, lack of love, lack of *agape*" (34). Stiker argues that the need for ritual purity is replaced by love: "The religious is first of all the bond among human beings, as it is first of all the love that unites God to [humanity]" (34). Individuals and the community as a whole can be healed and can enter into the Kingdom only when the dignity and the right of disabled people to fully partake in religious and social life are recognized (35).

Although disability rights activists currently often emphasize the integrity of disability to a person's life experience, a common discriminatory attitude reduces people labelled as disabled to one ostensibly defective trait. Hence, for example, a person with paraplegia becomes "the paraplegic," with all the attached stereotypical presumptions an observer brings to such a label. Once labelled as "the" paraplegic, all other traits and personal complexities become inconsequential. The individual with a "defect" *becomes* the defect, the defective person, less than human. Once a person is interpreted as subhuman, even unconsciously, inhuman treatment is justified or simply overlooked. When our eldest daughter used a wheelchair, it was common for strangers to speak to those who were with her rather than addressing her directly. They presumed that because she could not walk, she was not able to do anything else, either.

In Mark's Gospel, each instance of Jesus' miraculous healing separates the person from the infirmity. The infirmity itself is personified, reflecting a tradition of belief that an illness was a distinct entity invading a body. In the case of the demoniac, the demon is directly addressed and ordered to "come out of him!" (1:25). In other words, the demon and the man are not identical; the man is distinct from his infirmity. Peter's mother-in-law is lying with a fever, but when Jesus helps her up, "the fever left her" (1:31). She is not the fever. In the healing of the many, they, too, were "possessed with demons" (1:32); when the demons are expelled (1:34), the people return to health. Even in the case of the leper, whose identity is solely claimed by his disease, "Immediately the leprosy left him, and he was made clean" (1:42). Only the story of the paralytic in Capernaum deviates from this illness/body split. The man, not the paralysis, was commanded to walk. Initially, Jesus forgives the man's sins—demonstrating that though he is paralyzed, divine grace is still bestowed on him. This act elicits outrage from the scribes, who view the paralysis as a sign of divine disfavour. Jesus heals the man's paralysis in order to demonstrate his own authority: "So that you may know that the Son of Man has authority on earth to forgive sins …" (2:10). Jesus' actions show that the borders to divine graciousness patrolled by the religious authorities are in fact creations, constructs, of those authorities. Divine grace, imparted by Christ, knows no barriers.

These miracle healings of Jesus are often interpreted as a source for the pernicious association of disability with sin. Forgiveness of sins results in cure, suggesting that cure is a prerequisite for salvation; in short, disability is equated with damnation. Yet these accounts describe encounters of human relationship between Jesus and people with a disabling condition. The sins of the paralytic are forgiven because all people are sinners. The story depicting Jesus' bestowal of salvific grace on the paralytic despite crowds surrounding Jesus seeking the same for themselves illuminates the human integrity of the disabled man. He reaches Christ only because his friends rally around him, lowering him through the roof of the impossibly crowded house. Clearly, he is valued by his friends; not everyone marginalizes the paralyzed man. This account, together with the other stories of healing in Mark, highlight the humanity of the disabled individuals and Jesus' acknowledgement of their personhood and their faith. Disability does not impede a person's relationship with God and hence her or his ability to enter the Kingdom.

These miracle accounts illustrate a transformative process of inclusion into a community of God that requires relationships of respect and caring for all people, regardless of social identities. Biblical scholar Elisabeth Schüsler Fiorenza emphasizes the radical nature of this vision of the Kingdom:

> G*d's vision of a renewed creation entails not only a "new" heaven but also a "renewed," qualitatively different earth freed from kyriarchal exploitation and dehumanization. To articulate ekklesia, i.e., the assembly of full citizens, means to name an alternative reality of justice and well-being for all, without exception. (27)

Jesus' proclamation deliberately seeks to include those whose condition removes them from the mainstream. Jesus honours those who are unable to enter the church by the stairs or secure a position on the parish executive without unconventional accommodation.

Despite the Gospel inscriptions of Jesus' persistent inclusion of the socially marginalized, our communities often fail to reflect this openness. Our own experience, as well as what we have learned from other people who have a family member with a disability, reveals a serious lack of welcome and accommodation of difference in Christian communities.

Most wounding is a notion that the disabled person and her or his family are divinely punished for wrongdoing. The prejudice of defect imposed by society is intensified by a stigma of moral and spiritual transgression imposed by the faith community, which is positioned to provide the support described in the prophetic texts. This support often transmogrifies in church communities to self-righteous pity and charity, if not outright exclusion. The families as yet unaffected by disability "thank God" for "his goodness," feeling, of course, that they have earned their privilege by clean living, good genes, hard work, or whatever the current myth of success might be. They easily thank God for not being "special" like *that* family with *that* child. In this simplistic but all too familiar profile, the families likely would not get to know each other well enough to know each other's names. The family with the disabled member bears the mark of the leper in the Levitical codes, avoided for fear of contamination.

Luke: Overcoming the Curse of Physiognomy

We need to examine reasons for the Christian tradition's linking of illness and disability with sin and divine judgment. This perspective reflects a widely held ancient view that there was an inner coherence between one's spiritual state and one's physical condition. This association emerges in the Priestly writings on ritual purity. It is a perspective that continued to have its adherents in the first centuries of the Common Era. Mikeal Parsons argues that the late centuries before the Common Era and the first century of the Common Era were dominated in the Roman world by a physiognomic approach to understanding humanity. Physiognomy is a philosophy that describes physical traits as indicators of the character of the inner soul (Parsons, 18f.). This philosophy informed the Judaic tradition that believed physical blemishes of priests created blemished sacrifices (40) and underlay the Qumran community's absolute identification of physical blemish with spiritual blemish (42). Early Christianity developed within this culture, in which physiognomy was a dominant current. Significantly, writers such as Paul and Luke resist this approach to humanity (64). Paul, for example, recognizes that he should not be condemned for his physical shortcomings: "I who am humble when face to face with you, but bold towards you when I am away … Indeed, we live as human beings, but we do not wage war according to human standards … Look at what is before your eyes" (2 Cor. 10:1, 3, 7). Parsons argues that Luke is even more overt in challenging the dominance of a physiognomic approach.

> Luke refuses to exclude anyone from the social body of this eschatological community on the basis of the shape of the physical body … Luke introduces traditional understandings of physiognomy only to undermine them. No one is excluded from the eschatological community on the basis of his or her looks, and *this* is the message regarding physiognomy that Luke wishes to teach. (82)

The implications of this Lucan subversion of contemporary norms are critical. In Acts 3:1-10, "a man lame from birth" is brought to the gate of the Temple to beg for alms. We see an image of a man with damaged limbs, trapped in liminality, incapable of entering on his own, watching the legs of mobile worshippers passing through the entrance. When Peter and John approach the Temple, they neither ignore nor dismiss him. They have no alms to give him, but instead offer the message of Christ. Disability does not preclude hearing the call to salvation. The man's miracle cure symbolizes his response to the apostles: their preaching enables his entry into the Temple to praise God. Interpreting this passage as a devaluation of disability—presuming that the man could not enter the sacred space of the Temple *unless* cured—is not substantiated by the text and its symbolic structure. Had John and Peter carried the man through the gate, the symbolic weight of the image would suggest that the apostles forced the man's faith. What is remarkable is that they did not pass by the beggar, as those inside the Temple must have done. They offered their teaching to the outcast, who accepted the Word that enabled him to join the community of believers in Christ.

Similarly, the description of Zacchaeus in Luke 19 emphasizes a body and an occupation that would warrant exclusion by contemporaries. Despite being "short of stature" (v. 3) and a reviled tax collector, Zacchaeus responds to Jesus' personal call. Just as the beggar accepts an invitation to enter the sacred space of the Temple, so, too, Zacchaeus accepts Jesus' entry into his life. "Today salvation has come to this house, because he too is a son of Abraham" (v. 9). Luke's message is straightforward:

> "God shows no partiality" (Acts 10:34). Consequently, the covenant messianic community, the "whole" body of Christ, includes even—

perhaps especially—those who do not themselves have, in the eyes of the larger culture, a "whole" body. The kingdom of God belongs to these, and they to God's covenant community. (Parsons, 145)

Nonetheless, Parsons observes that later Christian writings often reflect, instead of resist, a physiognomic perspective. Thus the second-century text *The Acts of Paul* painstakingly describes Paul's physical appearance based on how the contemporary culture would expect a "military leader" to look (53). A Christian anthology, *Physiologus*, mistakenly ascribed to Jerome (c. 347–420) and Ambrose of Milan (339–397), exemplifies the physiognomic approach of the day. "The *Physiologus* enjoyed popularity throughout the late antique and early medieval periods, despite its condemnation as heretical by Pope Gregory" (58). As portrayed, Ambrose fell prey to the physiognomic impulse. Ambrose is convinced that bodily gestures reflect moral character. In one instance, he refuses ordination to a candidate because of "unseemly gestures" (59). In another instance, "Ambrose refuses fellowship with one already ordained because of the 'arrogance of his gait'" (59). In the face of this cultural current, Paul's self-reflections in his second letter to the Corinthians come into relief. Paul revels in his weakness: "I am content with weaknesses, insults, hardships, persecutions, and calamities for the sake of Christ; for whenever I am weak, then I am strong" (2 Cor. 12:10).

Rather than trying to argue against the physiognomic association of weakness and sin or immorality, he secures his weakness to grace. Furthermore, he associates weakness, or self-deprecation, with Christ. In his letter to the Philippians, Paul communicates the profound image of the "kenotic" or self-emptying God:

who, though he was in the form of God,
    did not regard equality with God
    as something to be exploited,
but emptied himself,
    taking the form of a slave,
    being born in human likeness.
And being found in human form. (2:6-7)

Even though physiognomic ideology is fundamentally unchristian in its denial of human complexity and in its reification of bodies as categorical objects, physiognomic belief persists throughout later Christian thought, perpetuating the oppressive association between ostensibly defective bodies and defective souls. Nevertheless, despite the duration of these pernicious myths, the biblical texts and Christian tradition continue to teach the wonder of creation in all its diversity and call all humanity to include each other in a collective embrace, acknowledging our interconnection and our need for each other.

Paul Rejoices in His Weakness

This interpenetration of the created and uncreated and the interconnectedness of weakness with glory is nowhere more evident than in the very person of Jesus Christ. Paul's Kenotic Christ is not only a symbol of the Suffering Servant, but is also the one who embraces weakness, brokenness, impoverishment, and disability both in his relationships and in his body. The Jesus story is a story in which leading players are those who are vulnerable, ill, disabled, and marginalized by their community. Jesus' ongoing tension with society's powerful arises from his unwillingness to leave the marginalized on the margins. Instead, he recognizes the lepers, the woman with an issue of blood, the lame, the blind. He embraces them, because he is one of them: "So marred was his appearance, beyond human semblance … he had nothing in his appearance that we should desire him" (Is. 52:14; 53:2). Paul recognizes the wonder of Christ's limitless encompassment and consequent sanctification of enfleshed human living: "'… for power is made perfect in weakness.' So, I will boast all the more gladly of my weaknesses, so that the power of Christ may dwell in me" (2 Cor. 12:9-10).

A habit of disrupting expectations of a constructed normalcy seems to culminate in a shameful criminal's death by crucifixion. However, Jesus's persistent transgression of social norms of exclusion set the stage for the ultimate irony of the Cross. Christ's embrace of human reality includes death, thereby even then disrupting expectations and transgressing mortality's horror with hope. The sign of a criminal's punishment becomes the "Holy, Precious and Life-giving Cross" (Eastern Christian proper). Death is allied with resurrection, with eternal life. Paul provocatively asks, "Where, O death, is your sting?" (1 Cor. 15:55). Jesus' broken body becomes a sign of eternal life, not of suffering or frailty.

The Resurrection does not signal a transcendence of humanity and gritty human reality. In context with the day-to-day living of Jesus of Nazareth, the Resurrection instead signals a celebration of divine love known through the fullness of being human, without margins. The Resurrection accounts emphasize Jesus' body as broken, wounded. We do not encounter a classic image of physical perfection but rather a body abused and impaired by dominant forces of power. Thomas's disbelief is taken away when he recognizes Jesus' broken body: "Put your finger here and see my hands. Reach out your hand and put it in my side. Do not doubt but believe" (Jn. 20:27). Christ's kenosis is complete and pivotal to his divine mission: brokenness, disability is not a subtraction from wholeness. Essentially, "brokenness" is not diminishment; it is salvific and fundamental to the human–divine relationship, to the newly established *koinonia*. The true human community is built upon the One whose body was broken for the sake of love. To be in relationship with God, then, is to recognize one's brokenness and so to share in the community of solidarity created by Christ's Cross. The notion of "unbrokenness," then, is merely an idea that varies according to context and relationship, just as having a disability may or may not be disabling for an individual.

The Church reaches out to those in need. We have ministries to the poor and ministries to the homeless, but do we reach out to those marginalized by disability prejudice? We don't need to put in an elevator because we don't have any parishioners in wheelchairs. We don't need to offer Eucharist to the person with an intellectual disability because he or she can't understand anything. Because Aleksandra has a priest for a father, her condition was quickly, broadly known. All of a sudden, people were confiding to us about the sisters, uncles, mothers, and children with disabilities who were kept secret, hidden from the community because they would not fit in. Family members were unable to fight the "border guard" of social stigma to bring them into the community. Where is the outreach of the People of God?

5

Embracing the Radical:
Early Christian *Koinonia*

As Christians, as followers of Christ, we are called to build a community of faith where we value one another, not for any instrumental worth we might have, but because we fundamentally need each other to share our being in God. We turn now to the notion of *koinonia* in order to explore this powerful charge to be creators of truly inclusive community.

There are, admittedly, many ways in which Christ's call to *koinonia* or community has been received. Some have seen it as a quasi-socialist call to building an egalitarian society. Others have perceived it as an invitation to a society of the elect—only for those who are morally or theologically pure. The varying understandings are not reflective of competing claims, we believe, but rather expressions of the very potency of Christ's call. The call is not univocal, evoking one possible response, because it is a call into a relationship. The community of believers in Christ, his apostles and disciples, is bound by a common person to whom all are related: the person of Jesus Christ. This foundational relationship and bond are rooted in an unmerited gift: Christ's offer of himself in love to all. But this offer, for the Christian, is also merely an indicator of a greater offer: the divine invitation into communion with the Triune God, who is relationship itself. The basis of both these relationships is the foundation of life itself: all have been called into existence by this Triune God, not as an expression of power or of experimentation, but of love. We and all creation have been primordially loved, even in "our mother's womb" (Ps. 50/51). The human community of believers is primarily constituted not by some code or even by a dogmatic statement—and least of all by a set of rules and regulations—but by this divine love and our free response to it. The ancient Christian text *The Didache* outlines the conviction of this early Christian community:

> There are two ways, one of Life and one of Death ... The Way of Life is this: Firstly, you must love the God who made you, and second, your neighbour as yourself. And whatever you want people to refrain from doing to you, you must not do to them. (1:1-2)

The Christian Gospel, too, tells us how to live. Life is to be lived in a loving response to divine love and then extended to those others who have been likewise loved: all of humanity. This powerful message of Christ, received and lived by the early Christian communities, does not represent a break with Jesus' own Judaic heritage. Rather, the message is deeply rooted in Israel's experience of the Lord and the powerful call of the greatest prophets.

Israel is the people of God not because of their own actions or merits, but by the graciousness of the Lord. In other words, it is a community called into being by the One who has loved Israel since before its birth. The Christian community is likewise a community that is called into being, not constituted by its own actions or decisions.

This fundamental giftedness of the true community is first portrayed in the story of the visitation of Abraham and Sarah (Gen. 18). The aged couple are visited by three angels (foreshadowing the Trinity) who prophesy that Sarah will bear a son, despite her age. The suggestion is so beyond belief that Sarah "laughed" at the prospect (Gen. 18:12). Nonetheless, the prophecy is repeated and magnified, now in the words of "the Lord": "Abraham shall become a great and mighty nation, and all the nations of the earth shall be blessed in him" (Gen. 18:18). Although this community/people is constituted by divine action, it also calls forth the faith and trust of Abraham and Sarah in welcoming the strangers into their home. Thus community, while a gift, is fulfilled in the hospitality that lies at its core:

the hospitality that does not see the stranger as someone to be feared or avoided but rather to be welcomed. The other, the stranger, is a blessing that moves the community into a greater way of being. The interchange, the relationship, is fruitful: it gives birth to a great "nation"—the people of God.

But in spite of this awareness of the Lord's goodness, which engenders Israel, Israel is not faithful to the relationship. The One who is reminds Israel of the bond of true community. Prophets are given to Israel to reawaken awareness of this bond. Isaiah was one of the greatest of these prophets. In his works, the Christian community hears the Lord's call for reform and recognizes the reality of human embodiment. The "Suffering Servant," who for Christians prefigures the person of Christ, is not the pretty Jesus character of Hollywood movies. Rather, his face is so disfigured that he is difficult to look upon (Is. 52:14-15). The Suffering Servant embodies the stigma linked to disability: causing disgust, shame, and sorrow. Yet the Suffering Servant embodies most completely the relationship between God and humanity, challenging us to look beyond our prejudices in building a new, fuller community than previously imagined. The Suffering Servant, in the person of Jesus Christ, reveals the meaning of true community: the God who is Trinity. This true community is the unity of the disparate and scattered: "as this piece [of bread] was scattered over the hills and then was brought together and made one, so let your Church be brought together from the ends of the earth into your Kingdom" ("Didache" 9:4).

Jean Vanier has often spoken about the person with an impairment as "gift." Aleksandra is a gift not only to her parents and siblings, but to all who meet her. She is a gift not only because of her brilliant eyes, sarcastic humour, and occasional but wondrous smile. She is a gift because she drools, because she cries out, because she keeps us up at night. She is a gift because she is who she is. Nothing more. We, too, are gifts, because we are who we are. She—we—do not need to prove ourselves, do not need to be income generators or taxpayers to be valuable human beings. We are valuable human beings simply because in our mother's womb, God called us by name. We are gift because the God of Love has loved us all.

6

Discovering Trinity:
Forming Christian Orthodoxy

lthough the Christian Scriptural tradition established the foundation for Christian teaching, what have come to be regarded as the essential elements of Christian faith were honed over subsequent centuries as a result of much conflict and debate. The first six or seven centuries after the Apostolic Period were of particular importance in this process. During this period, Christians tried to resolve perplexing issues of faith: What does it mean to say that Jesus is the Saviour? If Jesus saves, what does that mean for a monotheistic faith? How does Jesus save? If Jesus is human, what does that say about our humanity? How can we speak about Jesus and the Spirit as God? These questions and the proposed resolutions, many of which are still prescriptive for contemporary Christians, are critical to reconfiguring our attitudes towards disability.

Who Is This Man Jesus?

The first generations of the followers of Jesus were convinced that their experience of the Risen Lord had transformed them: they were living a new life; they were saved. The late first-century bishop of Antioch, Ignatius, taught that Jesus not only had created a new possibility for humanity after death, but equally significantly, Jesus opened up a new life for his followers in their present circumstance. "Christ means a new existence for the faithful, for they are 'members' of Christ … Through Jesus Christ, death is already overcome and life has been made present" (Grillmeier, 87). Somehow this man Jesus was the Saviour/Messiah/Christ: the one who both brought the possibility of eternal life and transformed the nature of our life in historical time. This life was no longer just about struggle and survival, it was about the possibility of a life-giving relationship with God through Jesus Christ and with all humanity through that same Christ. Irenaeus, Bishop of Lyons in the third century, saw Christ as "the exemplar and prototype of the image of God according to which man [sic] had been created" (Pelikan 1971, 145). The person of Jesus was the New Adam—a human being as we were meant to be.

But how was this possible if he was just the "son of Joseph"? If God had condemned humanity for its sinfulness, then must it not be God who releases humanity from the assigned judgment? For almost 300 years after the Resurrection, Christians struggled with and debated this question. Many Christians in these first centuries espoused Christ as Saviour, but at the expense of his humanity. Some, called Adoptionists, saw Jesus as a human being who was "adopted" by the Father at the baptism in the Jordan River (Lk. 3:22). For them, the baptism marked the union of a human and heavenly being. However, this Jesus was neither fully human nor fully God, ultimately not adequately expressing the Christian community's understanding of Jesus as Saviour.

Another movement within the Christian community that grappled with the nature of Jesus has been called Docetism (from the Greek word *dokeo*, to appear or seem to be). For the Docetists, Christ's humanity was a mirage, or mask, that the divine being (not necessarily God) put on to participate in the created order. The Docetists, and others who were called Gnostics, could not reconcile a divine being (from the non-material, spiritual realm) with one who could in fact suffer and die. The real historicity of the Jesus story was, in their minds, not possible if Jesus were Saviour and thus of the divine realm. Jaroslav Pelikan observes that "the very existence of docetism is also a testimony to the tenacity of the conviction that Christ had to be God, even at the cost of his true humanity" (Pelikan 1971, 174). Although this battle caused profound reverberations in the early Church, the underlying doubt about the real humanity of Christ continues to echo among many Christians today.

Nonetheless, in spite of the challenge that the humanity and, in particular, the suffering and death of Jesus created for the cosmology of the ancient Christian world, strong and consistent voices defended the real humanity of Jesus. Ignatius of Antioch, writing to the Trallians, asserts,

> Stop your ears, therefore, when any one speaks to you at variance with Jesus Christ, who was descended from David, and was also of Mary; who was truly born, and did eat and drink. He was truly persecuted under Pontius Pilate; He was truly crucified, and [truly] died, in the sight of beings in heaven, and on earth, and under the earth. He was also truly raised from the dead, His Father quickening Him, even as after the same manner His Father will so raise up us who believe in Him by Christ Jesus, apart from whom we do not possess the true life. (9)

Therefore, according to Ignatius, in acknowledging the humanity of Jesus and the reality of his death and Resurrection, one "possesses" true life. Other second-century teachers, such as Justin Martyr (103–165) and Melito of Sardis (died c. 180), similarly assert the importance of the humanity of Christ. Seeing in this humanity the full mediation between the Creator and the created, Melito even goes so far as to speak of Christ as "being at once God and perfect man." In the third century, Irenaeus of Lyons (c. 125–c. 202), the great challenger of the Gnostics and others whom he terms heretics, staunchly asserts the reality of Christ's flesh (Incarnation) and Passion (redemption). Irenaeus is adamant in emphasizing "the true incarnation of Jesus Christ and the true historicity of his act of redemption" (Grillmeier, 99). This means that Christ participated in every element of human life, thus demonstrating the falsehood of those who asserted that his humanness was just an appearance:

> He did not seem one thing while He was another, as those affirm who describe Him as being man only in appearance; but what He was, that He also appeared to be ... For He came to save all through means of Himself ... He therefore passed through every age, becoming an infant for infants, ... a child for children, ... a youth for youths, becoming an example to youths, and thus sanctifying

them for the Lord. So likewise He was an old man for old men … sanctifying at the same time the aged also, and becoming an example to them likewise. Then, at last, He came on to death itself, that He might be "the first-born from the dead, that in all things He might have the pre-eminence," the Prince of life, existing before all, and going before all. (391)

Thus, Jesus was the perfect human being: he "became what we are, that He might bring us to be even what He is Himself" (V, Preface). Later Christian theologians would take up this notion to argue even more strenuously for the divine goal of human existence. However, Irenaeus does give us an indication of what this new life through Christ involves, and it goes beyond moral rectitude. Christ is undoubtedly human, and most certainly divine, because it is through Christ that we see God "adoptively" and are led to the Father. In seeing God, we are then "in God, and receive of His splendour," and this splendour gives life—true life that is "fellow-ship with God … to know God, and to enjoy His goodness" (IV, XX: 5). Irenaeus and his forerunners do not present a comprehensive response to the questions about the divinity and humanity of Christ, but they do lay out the skeletal components of the forthcoming formulations of Christian orthodoxy. They provide vital elements for understanding disability in the human community. First, salvation for Christians does not entail the denial of humanity; rather, we are saved in and through our humanity. Second, humanity (demonstrated in perfection in Jesus Christ) involves all aspects of our earthly existence: suffering and death, all ages and circumstances of the human situation. Third, salvation and full humanity can be found only in relationship with God, a relationship that creates the paradigm for our relationship with each other.

How Can Christ Be Both Divine and Human?

Even though the formulations of Irenaeus and others clarified Christian teaching, they did not eliminate the contentious question of the divinity and humanity of Christ. This debate came to a head in the fourth century. Arius, an extremely popular preacher and cleric in Alexandria (Egypt), attempted to resolve the problem by proposing that Jesus, the Christ, was most certainly the bridge between the divine realm and the created realm, between God and humanity: related to both, but to neither fully. He wanted to avoid associating the Father and the Son too closely, arguing that Christ was created by God before all else: "the firstborn of all creation" (Col. 1:15). That meant "there was a time when the Son was not" (Socrates I: 5). Christ was the superlative creature and thus endowed with a unique role and power. He was the Saviour. Arius's position met with both widespread support and equally widespread condemnation, compelling Christian leaders to focus on this question: How do we speak about the relationship between Christ and the one true God?

Arius's argument was inviting because it was Scriptural and appeared to be reasonable, considering the logic of the day. Nonetheless, his language seemed to reduce the status of Christ to that of a "mere" creature, while not fully admitting his humanity. Arius's approach was consistent with Greek philosophical understandings of the Logos, but for many Christians it did not adequately respond to the weight of the experience of Jesus as the transformer of their lives and revelation of the Godhead. Arius's proposal forced the Christian community to clarify its understanding of Christ's humanity and his divinity. Despite failing to find adequate language to encompass Christ's humanity and Godliness, a strong Christian tradition could not accept Arius's portrayal of Christ as the most superlative creature.

The debate over Arius's language first came to a head in the Council of Nicaea in 325, but was only ultimately resolved at the Council of Constantinople in 381. A critical player in this debate was the church leader and sometime Bishop of Alexandria, Athanasius. His contribution to the formulation of the language of *homoousion*, meaning that Christ was of the same nature as God (of one essence and thus not created), is extremely well documented. However, what is of interest at this point is not so much the resolution as the arguments put forward. In particular, Athanasius contended that Christ had to be divine in order to be the Saviour: a creature cannot save a creature. Thus Christ could not be created. However, because God became human in Jesus, a startling aspect of human creation has been revealed:

> He became a human being that we might be divinized in him; he came to be in a woman and was begotten of a virgin in order to transport our errant race into himself and in order that from then

on we may become a holy race and "partakers of the divine nature." (2 Peter 1:4) ("Letter to Adelphius," 4, cited in Khaled, 238)

In coming to an understanding of Christ's divinity, Athanasius also expands our understanding of Christ's humanity and the purpose of human existence: to become like God, not by nature, but by adoption. Athanasius is consistent with and building upon the early Christian "image and likeness theology," which emphasizes that from the very moment that humanity was called into being, we were intended to grow in God-likeness ultimately to be with God for eternity, "partakers of the divine nature." Soon after Athanasius, another great teacher of the Church, Gregory of Nazianzus (c. 329–c. 389) deepens this profound understanding of humanity by asserting "that which He has not assumed He has not healed" (ci).

Fourth- and fifth-century Christianity came to clarify most profoundly that the Son of God took upon himself all things that are part of creatureliness/humanness, except for sin. However, the particular meaning of this assertion was developed only as we gradually expanded our understanding of what it meant to be human. When a society perceives a certain race, social status, or gender as inferior, the privileged centre is interpreting the profound call to be God-like as applying only to themselves: the elite. As we delve into our corporeal nature to encounter its complexity, diversity, and vicissitudes, we experience God in us and with us. We are who we are because of who God is.

Historically, Christians have reflected varying societal understandings of the human condition. Disputes have arisen over the inclusion of people with disabilities in communities. If Baptism requires intellectual assent, can someone who is intellectually impaired be baptized? Should someone who is unable to walk independently be an ordained minister in a community? Some Christian communities that strongly associate marriage with procreation deny that sacrament to those who are unable to engage in sexual intercourse. While Christian groups no longer restrict participation in the community based on gender or race, restrictions still are enforced against people with disabilities, in effect denying their personhood and implying that Christ has not "assumed" and hence not "saved" their way of being human.

The early debates about the *homoousion* formula defended by Athanasius gave way to new semantic sparring in the fifth and sixth centuries. Although the inclusion of *homoousios* in the Nicene-Constantinopolitan Creed settled the question that Jesus was both human and divine, it did not determine how this was possible or what the implications were for our understanding of God; monotheism could not be abandoned, in spite of believing that Jesus was God. In arguing against Arius's thought and those who later represented the so-called Arian camp, a Syrian Bishop, Apollinarius (d. 390), developed an understanding of Jesus as God in opposition to stances in Antioch that emphasized Jesus' humanity and moral example. In Apollinarius's view, the Antiochene position posited a being with two natures. By focusing on the divinity of Jesus, whose humanity lacked a human soul/mind, Apollinarius believed that he preserved the unity of Jesus' person. Neither the Antiochene position nor Apollinarius's elaboration brought unanimity to the Christian community; what one emphasized, the other only weakly affirmed. The two positions became even more extreme and adversarial through the work and relationship of Cyril of Alexandria (c. 376–444) and Nestorius of Constantinople (c. 386–c. 451). Their inflammatory polemic brought the Byzantine Empire to the brink of civil war. Although, after Cyril's death, Eutyches, a priest of Constantinople (380–456), continued to dispute the Nestorian position, he was ultimately condemned for heresy by the Council of Chalcedon in 451: he had argued that Jesus' humanity was somehow different from our humanity, thus jeopardizing the salvific import of Christ's Incarnation so powerfully argued by Athanasius and Gregory of Nazianzus. That same Council proclaimed a singular formula for understanding the relationship between humanity and divinity in Jesus: two natures (divine and human) united, without commingling in one divine person. While many Christians rejected this Chalcedonian formula, by the early 21st century we understand that it clarified Christian orthodoxy's defence not only of the divine unity of the Father and the Son, but also of Jesus as the complete and undeniable immanence of God in the fullness of humanity. The Anglican theologian T.F. Torrance writes,

> God is God and not man, and yet in the incarnation God has become man, this particular Man, Jesus Christ, without ceasing to be God. In Him divine nature and human nature are united, really

and eternally united, in one Person. In Him the eternal Word of God has assumed human nature and existence into oneness with Himself in order thus, as truly divine and truly human, to become the final Word of God to man and the one Mediator between God and man. In other words, the incarnation shows us that God reveals Himself (God) in terms of what is not-God (man) …. (15)

Thus it is in our humanity, our very diverse and vulnerable humanity, that God reveals Self; in and through that very diverse and vulnerable humanity, we come to know God. When we allow ourselves to confront the magnitude of the notion that all humanity is divinized through Christ's humanity, we can begin to recognize the folly of our automatic enculturated bigotries that compel us to reject individuals from a fear of their perceived difference, be it in status, gender, ability, age, etc. Nancy Eisland articulates this astonishing revelation as the disabled God in the volume of the same name: not a God of Olympian power and might, but the God who lives in loving connection with human beings, venturing to "rub shoulders" with those human beings whom society would at best relegate to restricted spaces, away from the centres of social vibrancy.

Christ Assumes Our Humanity in Its Entirety

Today, when we regard someone as "special" or with "special needs," we, albeit unconsciously, push them away from the "all" of humanity, diminishing their roles as equally divinized humans. At the same time, we distance ourselves from Christ. How? Our refusal to be open to the "foreignness" of another closes us off to the complex realities of our own selves. Without encountering our human realities, we avoid encountering Christ. God's power is manifest in the fleshly dependencies of a person whose refusal to conform to socio-cultural norms results in alienation, degradation, and a criminal's death. Christ embodies human frailty together with the bold strength of human love. Through Christ we know God.

This vision of God is the core revelation of the Incarnation. Inasmuch as the developing Christian tradition discovers a new understanding of humanity, it expands its understanding of God. The gradual confirmation of Jesus' divinity and recognition of the Spirit as divine leads to the unique Christian form of monotheism: a Trinitarian or Triune God.

In establishing the humanity and divinity of Jesus in the fourth and fifth centuries, the Christian community opened up a unique quandary. How do you continue to distinguish one God when you speak of a Father, a Son, and a Holy Spirit—all God? We probably owe the greatest debt to the Cappadocians (Macrina the Younger [330–379], Basil the Great [330–379], Gregory of Nazianzus, and Gregory of Nyssa) for articulating what today is regarded as the orthodox teaching on the Trinity. Basing their argument for the divinity of the Spirit, equal to the Father and the Son, on the words of the baptismal formula (a Christian is baptized into the name of the Father, and of the Son, and of the Holy Spirit) (Pelikan 1971, 217), the Cappadocians established a Trinitarian faith as fundamental Christian orthodoxy. In essence, they maintained that although the three divine persons are one God and thus one, they are distinguishable not by any individual characteristics, but by their relationship. What you say about the Father you can say about the Son, except that the Father is the Father and the Son is the Son. Similarly, what you say about the Son, you can say about the Spirit, except that the Spirit is the Spirit and the Son is the Son. Thus God, the divine Persons, are not defined by what they do, how they act, or how they "appear," but rather by how they relate one to the other. The doctrine of the Christian Trinity establishes relationship as an ontological category of being. The Father is the origin, or *monarchos*; the Son is the only-begotten (*monogenes)* of the Father; and the Spirit is the one who proceeds/spirates (*ekporeusin*) from the Father. All three are equal and without origin, for the Father cannot be Father without the Son, and the Spirit cannot be the Spirit of God, unless proceeding from the Father and resting on the Son. Thus Gregory of Nyssa was able to say that the Trinity is marked not by partnership, but by unity (Pelikan 1993, 246). Basil established this unity as "a oneness in nature but not in number" (246). This Trinitarian mystery stands at the heart of the Christian message and fulfills the promise of the incarnation: through Christ, the Son of God, we come to know God and the fullness of divine life.

Maximus the Confessor: Synthesizing the Tradition

Maximus the Confessor (c. 580–662) recognizes the intimate relationship between the Trinitarian revelation and the entry of God into human flesh. His work most profoundly speaks of the Incarnation revealing the

Trinity, creating "the most wonderful Christological synthesis of the ancient Church" (Schönborn, 102).

In coming to know the Incarnate One, we do not simply "know Jesus." We in fact engage the fullest revelation of the Divine Trinity—God in perfection. The Incarnation—the embodiment of the Son of God—therefore stands "as the heart of the divine design ... The Incarnation reveals the meaning and the destiny of all creation" (123). Thus the Incarnation is "no longer viewed as a mere pedagogical concession to human weakness, a concession to be surpassed by rising onto a higher level of knowledge" (123). The Incarnation reveals the true God, a God who wills

> the union of humanity and divinity in a paradoxical conquest, which does not transform or dissolve God into man or man into God, which rather renews human nature and imprints on it the mode of existence of the Eternal Son. This conquest, which leads human nature to its ultimate perfection, is called *love*. (123)

The loving relationships of the Trinity, revealed in and through Jesus Christ, are thus the model for human conduct—the goal of human life.

Yet this goal is not simply an eschatological one: awaiting our death and desired union with God in heaven. Rather, for Maximus, this love is at the core of the Christian life as lived in time, on earth. The divine *kenosis* in the Incarnation makes absolutely possible, if not necessary, human deification: "Man's deification is not only reciprocally related, but directly and quantifiably proportionate to the extent of God's humanization, and dependent upon it" (Cooper, 46). As we come to know God in Christ, we come to know ourselves and discover that we can be actualizers of divine love.

> The person "caught up" in the process of deification becomes an agent of divine manifestation in the ordered totality of his corporeal human nature ... And because God's deifying presence in his body is incarnated as love, it is as it were sacramentally effective: capable of binding both himself and other human beings to God. In other words, the deified subject himself, as God by grace, becomes a means of deifying others. (41)

For Maximus, Gregory of Nyssa's constant growth in perfection entails not just the individual, but of necessity engages others. Maximus does not limit this deifying agency to humanity but extends it to all existence: "Only in deified humanity do cosmos and Scripture attain their proper status and goal" (48). Enlightened by the deifying action of divine love, we come to realize the true nature of existence; that which previously seemed to be "other," disdained, feared, may now be recognized as manifesting the rich diversity inherent in all creation—reflective of the divine and so to be embraced and loved.

Maximus recognizes that oppositional binaries have permeated human understanding. This division is evident in the way humanity has constructed the divine–human relationship, the ultimate opposites. In the Incarnation, however, this opposition is reconciled: reconciled, but not dissolved. The Incarnate One is both human and divine—neither nature is subsumed or lessened by the other. This perfect (hypostatic) union, as we have said, reveals the perfect union of the Divine Trinity, bound by love. This union does not dissolve the difference of the three Persons but rather sustains it in a mysterious mutual indwelling (*perichoresis*), which Kallistos Ware describes as "an unceasing movement of mutual love" (1986, 11). As a result, Maximus argues that the apparent oppositions in creation are not elements of the divine design, but rather are the product of the Fall.

> Opposition reigns when the free will clearly moves contrary to reason and contrary to its natural disposition; difference, on the other hand, results from the operation of nature acting in harmony with its natural disposition. Opposition is a revolt against a nature, while difference undergirds this nature. (cited in Schönborn, 125–26)

Just as Christ, the God-Human (*theanthropos*), has united the divine and the human, so now humanity, through love, can reconfigure that which has been seen as opposite and recognize difference without opposition. According to Lars Thunberg, "Unity without annihilation is the supreme divine goal" (76).

Although Maximus delineates only a five-fold mediation (created–uncreated; intelligible–sensible; heaven–earth; paradise–this world; masculine–feminine), his premise is clear: difference does not mean opposition. Christ, the Incarnate One, has "recapitulated in Himself all things, showing that the whole creation is one … achieved through the coming together of all its members" (cited in Thunberg, 90). Thus the very opposition that disability manifests—an opposition between those who are "able" and powerful versus those who are "disabled" and powerless—is the result of sin. The Christian and the Christian community must admit "difference" (we differ, each individual from the other), but we must not allow difference to transmogrify into opposition. Difference is a central characteristic of the human condition and so at the very core of human community when united in love. In fact, Maximus sees love (*caritas*) as the essential way in which deification is manifested: "In this state of charity all are loved equally and indeed it is but one and the same love which we extend to God and man" (Sherwood, 93).

Again, reflecting the paradox of the Incarnation, this love is not simply a human activity, but rather, as a deifying action, it is a divine–human (*theandric*) activity. "It implies the perfect unification of all that is naturally and positively human, as well as its transcendence, going beyond this dimension as such" (Thunberg, 108). Thus, the Christian and the Christian community have a particular responsibility to reject the construction of disability as opposition: "Love of those who know only hatred and hostility is the first step to liberation from the very things that stand as obstacles in the path toward imitating the God who loves all people equally" (Cooper, 249). Hence, for followers of Christ, there can be no "us and them"; there can be no "other" to be erased within the labyrinth of social service systems. Interconnection with those marked as other by society is an imperative for one who embodies Christ, for one who grows in knowledge of the Triune God.

Maximus's thought recalibrates our understanding of the Christian tradition. He receives and endorses the accepted power of the Cross as a sign of Christ's *kenotic* love. However, Maximus avoids interpreting the Cross and Christ's self-giving as a ransom or repayment to the Father. He does not endorse stoic forbearance in the face of suffering and challenges those who believe that suffering is a form of divine judgment or a demand of divine satisfaction. Maximus sees in the passion of Jesus something more profound and reflective of the divine mystery: the archetypal expression of the divine–human synergy. "Bodily suffering has no merit in itself … Even the Saviour became a human being 'not to suffer, but to save'" (Cooper,

242–43). Maximus's view on Jesus in the Garden of Gethsemane focuses not on a God who desires the death of the Son, but rather on the Son who anguishes over death yet resolutely understands the cost of living truth in love. The demand of love is not death or suffering; it is faithfulness. However, the misguided (constructed and destructive) norms of this world are such that this faithfulness, this love, will result in suffering and death (literal or figurative).

Too often, non-disabled church members will sadly concede that everyone has a "cross to bear," ostensibly encouraging the person marked by disability to emulate Christ stoically. This view misrepresents the meaning of the Cross and the Incarnation as a whole. The "suffering" of the person with a disability, if it exists, is hardly an occasion for holiness. Disabling someone whose body or mind has limitations is not caused by a person's sin or divine judgment; it results from our inability as individuals and as community to express *caritas* (love for one another). Disability, like the Cross, is not a sign of a vengeful God, but rather the result of a world enveloped by sin—propagating opposition and fragmentation rather than diversity and community. Jesus' response in the Garden is not a lesson to the one marked as disabled, but to all those who disable. The divine will calls us to *caritas*, to live the life of the Trinity.

Augustine of Hippo: Focusing on the Oneness of God

So far, our reflections on disability and Trinity have centred on key theologians of the Christian Church from the eastern part of the ancient Roman Empire. Christians of the West may be more familiar with Augustine of Hippo (354–430), the eminent bishop and teacher. Rereading the work of Augustine also offers valuable insight into our Christian heritage and our attitudes towards people with disability labels. Augustine's influence on Western Trinitarian thought is second to none; for many, "Augustine is often treated as the source and exemplar of a distinctively western style of trinitarian theology" (Ayres, 51). For these readers, Augustine's approach is exemplified by a focus on the divine unity that is reflected by analogy in the internal operations of the human mind. For this reason, unity–singularity, not Trinitarian diversity, becomes the dominant paradigm for the Church and human community. Similarly, the purported Augustinian emphasis on interiority privileges human rationality and the imagined perfections of Platonic forms, and identifies the image of God with human reason. Stephen McKenna concludes that "to Augustine it seemed better to begin with the unity of the divine nature, since this is a truth which is demonstrated by reason" (cited in Gunton, 35). Consequently, the theological tradition of the Christian West has related knowledge of God with the unity of God's essence, thereby subordinating the relationship of Divine Persons. Trinity becomes a secondary concept.

Karl Rahner has observed, "It looks as if everything that matters for us in God has already been said in the treatise *On the One God*" (cited in Gunton, 35). Ostensibly, Augustine's emphasis on divine unity is in significant tension with the relational emphasis so evident in theologians of the East. Gunton concludes that "Augustine is taking a clear step back from the teaching of the Cappadocian Fathers" (44). Therefore many Orthodox and Western scholars alike believe "we have relatively little to learn from Augustine in the task of constructing a properly 'relational' model of God's trinitarian life" (Williams, 317). In fact, Augustine's theology has been charged with even greater offenses than neglecting Trinitarian theology.

> Augustine stands accused of collaborating in the construction of the modern consciousness that has wrought such havoc in the North Atlantic cultural world, and is busy exporting its sickness to the rest of the globe, while occluding the vision of the whole planet's future in its delusions of technocratic mastery—a hugely inflated self-regard, fed by the history of introspection. (317)

All this misdirection is judged to have arisen from Augustine's apparent emphasis on divine oneness. Furthermore, this error has been instrumental in constructing models of unity in the Christian Church that diminish or even eliminate diversity, that prescribe authority as singular rather than communal, and that value introspective emulation of the divine life over lived Christian community. However, recent scholarship argues that traditional interpretations of Augustine are ill conceived and therefore that blaming him for consequent developments in the Christian West is unjustified.

In the past few decades, a number of scholars have demonstrated that Augustine's Trinitarian theology is much closer to that of the Cappadocians than had been presumed, and that the relationality of the three persons of the Trinity is indeed central to his work. Rowan Williams argues that "Augustine's reflection on the trinitarian being of God opens up theological possibilities very different from the proto-Cartesian or proto-Kantian tendencies with which he has been charged" (318). Williams interprets a powerfully relational view of Trinity in Augustine. He highlights Augustine's own affirmation: "there is no 'divinity' not constituted by the act of 'caritas'" (325). This loving God creates relationship at the very instant of our creation, at the core of our being—the relationship itself is the image of God. Thus, being the image of God is "a matter of *relation* to God (and of charity realised in us by the Holy Spirit); it also depends upon the belief that the God who is imaged himself wills relation by imparting his own life" (321).

Growing in the image of God, then, does not entail an abandonment of our humanness or createdness, but rather necessitates a being "at home with our created selves (ourselves as produced, derived) … The image of God in us might be said to entail a movement into our createdness, because that is a movement into God's own life as turned 'outwards'" (321). Other scholars have joined Williams in calling for a fuller exploration of Augustine's contribution to Trinitarian theology. Lewis Ayres sees Augustine's teaching on divine simplicity—"in God all qualities are identical with God's essence" (63)—as fundamental to a proper reading of his Trinitarian thought. Ayres argues that

> if we consistently apply this grammar [of divine simplicity] to the principles of trinitarian theology, then the natural conclusion of this generation is that the three persons must be both distinct and also one in unity of existence and wisdom itself … Such language draws us to the individual reality of the persons and then *immediately* to their unity, without the need to imagine a substance or something which provides that linkage. (66)

Thus unity is neither a pre-condition of Trinity nor an underlying superior reality. Rather, Augustine, too, moves from the personal relationships to the Triune essence: "The triune communion *is* a consubstantial and eternal unity; but there *is* nothing but the persons" (67). Finally, Ayres concludes, Augustine's reputation for privileging the divine unity at the expense of diversity cannot be substantiated. Although not yet fully scrutinised, these interpretations suggest more consistency in Augustine's approach with those of the Eastern teachers than previously recognized. Similarly, Augustine has been decried for having so emphasized human rationality and intellect that the subsequent Western reception of his thought has marginalized people with intellectual disabilities. Current scholarship sees Augustine as simply reflecting the ambiguity of many early Christian thinkers: on the one hand affirming the acceptance and equality of all human beings in the eyes of God, and on the other hand expecting the inferior treatment of many as an unavoidable consequence of human sin (Stainton, 494). Augustine's emphasis on the individual's need for grace muted his vision of a Christian message that extends beyond the individual to the community, a community that should be transformed in the image of the co-equal and mutually indwelling Triune God.

Trinity Is the Key

There is no doubt that attempts to conceptualize the perfect relationship of three persons who are one being boggle the mind. Even Basil the Great declared that "what was common to the Three and what was distinctive among them lay beyond speech and comprehension and therefore beyond either analysis or conceptualization" (Pelikan 1971, 223). However, symbols and images enhance communication and comprehension. Eastern Christian iconography facilitates recognition of the reality of the Trinity visually and symbolically through the representation of the previously discussed biblical narrative of the visitation of Abraham and Sarah. For Christians, this story prefigures the revelation of the Trinity. Rublev's icon of the Trinity, currently among the most popularly replicated icons the world over, depicts three angels seated around a circular table—the altar, the Sanctuary. Although coloration of the figures differs, they are virtually indistinguishable. They sit around the table, forming an open circle that is completed only by the viewer. Their hands point to the other, forming another circle. The scene, therefore, is one of unity and harmony, defined by the interrelatedness of the three figures, as well as their implicit invitation to the viewer to enter into the relationship, into the Sanctuary, by completing the circle: the Holy Trinity. Synchronically, we who are in the image and likeness of that Trinity are defined as well: we are potential participants in the Trinitarian relationship. Humanity participates in the "community of being" that is the divine Trinity (Zizioulas).

The Divine Trinity offers a radical challenge to our desire for control and comfort. Forming communities based on relationships secured in love for others—because we ourselves feel so loved that we cannot help but love more—can sound zany, something akin to a 1960s love-in. Honestly, where does the financial support come from? Is there a musician to take charge of hymn singing? Who can work the kitchen? How about printing up weekly bulletins? The practical list is never ending. Certainly, in groups we need to be organized and we need organizers. We choose leaders and commit-tees to effectively run operations. This is inarguably practical and good. But when we reflect on driving principles of success in our communities, we find that there is little distinction between a well-run business and a popular church community. This in itself need not be problematic, but we would probably want to argue that the foundational values between church and business differ. Still, the organizations will look the same for the simple fact that we subconsciously operate according to the laws of a deeply entrenched ideology of normalcy. We conform or become invalid(ated). Unconsciously, our church communities tend to conform more to the tyrannical societal norm than to the dictates of Christ. But with conscious awareness, we can become the communities of love that drew people so compellingly to follow Christ in the nascent Christian Church.

In keeping with the irony of the Cross, the population most alienated by dictates of normalcy—those labelled "disabled"—is the population that currently holds the key to liberating our parishes from the shackles of society's rigid consumer mentality into the vibrant embrace of the living Trinity. Returning to the comparison of successful business to successful parish, we know that, although there may be other goals, businesses exist to make money. Why do parishes exist?

Amid the myriad complex answers to this question, there is one basic response: To follow Christ in order to know God. But this is not simply an individual responsibility. Why? Because Christ is God; God is love; love is relational; God is diversity; God is Trinity. We follow Christ by entering into the Trinity through a loving plurality of humanity. We depend on each other in our parish communities to be Christ-like and, like Christ, to celebrate and suffer our lives deeply and fully.

> Many years ago we were told to "put Aleksandra away." Had we done that, our lives would have been easier and our careers much more successful. We would have gained more in the eyes of our society. But we would have had to dissolve our relationship. We would have had to place "me" first. Relationships are not really planned. Nor are they judged on the balance of practical alternatives. Relationships are about love, sacrifice, humility, loss, tears, and joy. Through the Cross to Resurrection. Can we know God any other way?

7

Interdependent Living:
Models of Christian Community

Just as the first centuries establish the fundamental teachings of Christianity, they also provide models for Christian living. In spite of the scarcity of information on the community life of the first Christians, as mentioned earlier, we do know that the Deuteronomic call to love God and neighbour, as exemplified by Jesus, was central. The first Christians renounced the dominant values and norms of their society, and their co-religionists became their new family. This new family was a source of strength, encouragement, and support. Communities sought to manifest the Christian ideal with hospitality that emulated the embrace of humanity by a loving and forgiving God. It was the way of life to which the *Didache* called all faithful followers of Christ.

As the number of Christians grew, and they came to represent all sectors of the Greco-Roman world, it became more difficult for communities to practise the ideal. By the beginning of the fourth century, Christians had become such a significant force in the Mediterranean world that they became, ironically, the target of a massive generalized persecution. (Diocletian's Edict of 303 specifically withdraws the legal rights of anyone practising the Christian faith.) This was the final attempt by Roman authorities to destroy Christianity. Diocletian's efforts were soon eclipsed by the Edict of Toleration of 311 that formally ended the persecution. The Edict of Milan, 313, issued by Constantine, followed soon after, granting legal rights to Christians. Acceptance, preferential status, and, finally, in 380, the declaring of Christianity as the official religion of the Roman Empire (Edict of Thessalonica), meant that Christians now lived in an ostensibly Christian world—the *oikumene*.

Caring Means Relationship

But many Christians did not recognize this nominally Christian world as one that truly approximated the Gospel ideal. One way in which the norms of ancient Greco-Roman society differed from the aspirational norms of Christians was in the treatment of those marginalized due to sickness or infirmity. In Roman society, those who were sick were often blamed or held responsible for their state, whereas Christians voiced opposition to this perspective (Crislip, 70). The story of Zotikos, a fourth-century resident of Constantinople, marks this shift in understanding loving service (*caritas*). Zotikos represents a new Christian understanding of the relationship between the infirm and God. Rather than seeing the infirmity as punishment and the infirm in need of atonement, Zotikos demonstrates "a new attitude toward misfortune and suffering" (Stiker, 76), one based in recognizing the person in need as a "gift," a sign of divine creativity, and therefore to be cherished and supported. As early as the late first century, Ignatius of Antioch regarded the Christian community's concern for and support of those in need as "the distinguishing mark of the real Christian" (Crislip, 59). This ideal was not easily translated into reality in the newly declared "Christian" world, and voices arose calling for a more faithful adherence to the Gospel. For them, Christianity had to be lived more simply, more radically, and more in true community. These were the first monastics. Often, they lived alone, but always in some form of community association, even establishing communities of the faithful with a single purpose: coming to know God.

Much has been written about monastics seeking to separate themselves from other people, from "the world," in order to devote themselves to a solitary life of prayer and contemplation. The image of someone living for her or his own salvation, disconnected from others and their concerns, and even the root of the word "monastic"—*monos*, or one/alone—all suggest little connection between monasticism and a theology of community and Trinitarian interrelatedness. But the common stereotype of monasticism is far removed from the origins of the monastic movement. One of the first leaders of this movement is the Egyptian Pachomius (c. 292–346). The impulse for his conversion to Christianity is telling:

> While billeted in Thebes, he was impressed by the charity of local Christians, described to him as doing "all manner of good to everyone." "They treat us with love for the sake of the God of heaven." Pachomius then prayed to the Christian God, promising that he would serve his fellows in the same way. (Rousseau, 58)

For Pachomius, the call to Christianity and to monasticism did not lie in a search for solitude or an escape from a sinful world; rather, this call touched a desire to serve: to express the love of God. It was through service that Pachomius grew in his knowledge of God. It was "little more than basic Christianity" (63). Although at times he was misunderstood even by fellow monastics, Pachomius "acts above all else as a servant—preparing meals, caring for the sick, attending to the material side of life" (64).

The model of Pachomian monasticism, widely seen as the precursor of later monastic communities, was built around inclusive communities of mutual support and caring that recognized that through their interdependent community they would grow in knowledge of God. So much for the

> lingering misconception that monasticism, ancient and modern, is individualistic in its piety, that monks avoid at all costs contact with other people and the world. The truth is that monasticism, even eremitic, anchoritic monasticism, is essentially communal. The community is the body of Christ, and the heart of the community is eucharistic ... Ancient monasticism is fundamentally defined by *coming together* as a group, as a community, with a spiritual master, for the purpose of worshiping God. (Paphnutius, 26–27)

The community of the faithful mirrors the iconic Trinity of Rublev, who are gathered around the table and gathering others into the eucharistic assembly. In reflecting on early Egyptian monasticism, Tim Vivian concludes that "At the root of monastic spirituality lies hospitality, not just in the sense of *receiving* others, but in the sense of *reaching out* to others.

This is *hesychia*, and joined with it is prayer and the quiet handiwork of a contemplative life" (Paphnutius, 39).

Significantly, *hesychia*, or stillness, should not be confused with rejecting human community. Kallistos Ware asserts that true *hesychia* is about "men and women fully devoted to a life of service in the world who yet possess prayer of the heart; and of them it may justly be said that they are living the 'contemplative life'" (1975, 14). Thus the Christian life, whether monastic or not, involves love of neighbour, not in a general and nebulous sense, but rather through "personal involvement in the particular situation or need of another … it is activated in the concrete circumstances surrounding individual persons" (Aumann, 17). The image of Jesus reaching out to all around him as servant, not as master, is the true paradigm for the monastic, as it is for all Christians.

Caritas is not Charity

The imperative of service, practically engaging the other in love (true *caritas*), continued to be the focus for monastic development over the next centuries. Once more we turn to the Cappadocians and, most specifically, Basil of Caesarea. Basil was both a bishop and a very influential adapter of Pachomian monasticism, which has come to be known as cenobitic or communal monasticism. For Basil, the monastic life was not exceptional, but rather the natural expression of the Christian Gospel: the call to love. Because, according to Basil, prayer and service were indivisible in the life of a Christian, the life of the solitary could not mean a life without service to the neighbour:

> For Basil, the solitary life is a dangerous temptation, for the aim of the Christian life is love, whereas "the solitary life has one aim, the service of the needs of the individual", which is "plainly in conflict with the law of love" … But further, the solitary will have no one to correct him for his defects, and (what is perhaps for Basil the most serious point) the solitary will neither be able to share his spiritual gifts with others, nor benefit from theirs … For Basil the mutual support and correction provided only by a community are essential to the life of the monk. (Louth, 165)

It is in such a community that "all selfishness and self-reliance is set aside" (Pennington, 89), and so true Christian *koinonia* can be experienced by all. John Chrysostom describes this *koinonia* or fellowship as one in which "hospitality ... is not merely a friendly reception, but one given with zeal and alacrity, with readiness, and going about it as if one were receiving Christ Himself" (455). Therefore, this *caritas* is service done not in addition to faith, but clearly as the necessary extension of faith. It cannot be delegated to another. Once more, Chrysostom's admonition is significant: "Give not alms to those who preside in the Church to distribute. Bestow it thyself ... Give with thine own hands" (455).

Our modern construction of charity is clearly at odds with this earlier view of *caritas*. The former reflects a delegation of responsibility and a commodification of Christian service: we do not act ourselves to love our neighbour (in spite of our championing social justice), but rather we "pay" someone else to act. Much literature exists about the degrading nature of charity telethons in North America. In his essay "Conspicuous Contribution and American Cultural Dilemmas," the historian Paul Longmore describes the institutionalization of charitable giving in the United States as a process to verify one's worth as a successful American citizen who works strenuously to maintain a myth of self-sufficiency. He argues that economic success and personal health are equated with public virtue and are mandatory for equality. "Institutionalized charities manufacture 'the less fortunate' as status-enhancing commodities. Telethon giving, like all charitable donation and volunteerism, is on one level a corrective of the morally and communally corrosive effects of individualistic consumerism" (151). Charity, then, as opposed to *caritas*, is divisive, demeaning less fortunate individuals while raising the status and self-satisfaction of the affluent, permitting many donors to "confuse narcissism with empathy" (144). Conspicuous contribution assuages American guilt for abandoning the obligations of community and public welfare in order to practise conspicuous personal consumption. Charity offers the guise of altruism to selfish gains. Building on Longmore's analysis, we would add that public displays of charity, in purporting to "fix" disabilities through large contributions of money, also replace a dependency on God for miraculous cures; the fulfillment of miracle is taken on by the generous contributor who, as Longmore contends, "can still transcend the human condition ... all they have to do is take people with disabilities and make them over" (156). In contrast, the early Christian notion of *caritas* was direct and personal. It was not simply about "helping" another; it was about the quality and nature of the community we create and how it approximated the love of God, the love of the Trinity.

A Struggle Between Solitude and Service

This understanding of monasticism inspired the perspectives of many who followed: Augustine of Hippo, Benedict of Nursia (c. 480–547), Gregory the Great (540–604), and the medieval reforms of Francis of Assisi (1181–1226), Marie d'Oignies (1177–1213), and others. They all attempted to remind the Christian community that being a follower of Christ entailed both a deeply passionate life of prayer and a profoundly committed life of service. Their example challenges a trend that has given priority to the interior life, to the detriment of the communal. In the Middle Ages, with the rise of new monastic forms, especially in Western Christianity, a more "intellectualist view of the Christian life" (Tugwell, 299) took hold. This perspective had already been expressed in the writings of John Cassian (360–435), who believed that the solitary life is superior (although he did admit that such a life was possible only after learning service in the community). In the eleventh century, Peter Damian (1007–1072) developed the image of the monastic as "married" to Christ, expressing the relationship as an individual's act of love through a rejection of the world. Such a perspective devalued corporeality and service to others.

The association of spirituality with the mind, in opposition to physical needs and realities, led to practices of degradation of the flesh, such as voluntary self-flagellation (Miccoli, 472–74). This shift to privileging solitary introspection and subordinating the body and service to others came to dominate scholarship in later centuries. That is why Aquinas's theology is intellectual. Christian precepts become analytical exercises rather than vital actions. For Aquinas, the active Christian life garners value only in its contribution to spiritual introspection. "Aquinas shows that the active life may have an ascetical value as a preparation for contemplation, but it may have a mystical value of its own as when the apostolate flows from the perfection of charity and a deep interior life" (Aumann, 132).

The Medieval West embedded the idea of a superiority of intellect by derogating embodiment. Ironically, as the Church of the Middle Ages became progressively immersed in excessive wealth and moral laxity, this drive to interiority increased. Therefore, even an attempt at renewing and reforming the Church, as manifested in the work of Thomas à Kempis (c. 1380–1471), resulted in greater interiority: "the spiritual life is an interior life and … the most difficult battles must be waged within the confines of one's own soul" (Aumann, 165). This dichotomizing of interior/spiritual and exterior/bodily has profoundly influenced Christian development and Western intellectual thought to this day, and has contributed to the oppressive treatment of people whose disabilities draw extraordinary attention to corporeal realities. Many within the Christian tradition have emphasized that "charity is just as essential as Faith, [which] is indeed its fulfilment. Yet, concern for one seems to bring about a denial of the other" (Karam, 143). In part, this binary has produced a culture in which acts of pity (charity) parade as love of neighbour, occluding the imperative for a radically just *caritas* rooted in Christian solidarity and expressive of our common desire to mirror the divine community. Charity rooted in pity denigrates, whereas *caritas* is a function of divine love, a gift of the Holy Spirit.

The Fool for Christ's Sake

A unique and instructive manifestation of the power of the Holy Spirit is seen in the Holy Fool for the sake of Christ. Reminding us of the inherent falsity of seeing human community as homogenous, over the centuries and particularly in the Christian East, a cherished place has been preserved for those who manifest their love of neighbour through "excess, foolish intensity" (Saward, 46). The actions of these men and women are deemed as outrageous and scandalous by those around them. Examples include a nun evoking scorn and mockery from her community by feigning madness (Palladius's fourth-century nun), a monk visiting brothels at night to convert the prostitutes (Symeon), a man standing naked in public to manifest the hypocrisy of social values (Francis of Assisi). In all these instances, the Christian (not necessarily a monastic) acts contrary to social norms, shunning public approval, creatively embodying Christ's radical transformation of the natural world.

The fool, we notice, is a *stranger* … free from the normal ties of family life … homeless, a wanderer, often an exile … constantly in the company of his fellow humans. And yet he remains somehow an alien, an expatriate, on the margin of organised society, in the midst of the world yet not of it. The fool is free, a stranger—and therefore capable, as we shall see, of fulfilling a *prophetic* role. (Ware, 1984, 7)

But to what end, such madness? The Fool reminds the Christian community that the wisdom and norms of the world (even the Christian world of Byzantium or pre–20th-century Russia or Ukraine) are not the norms or wisdom of God. The Fool stands as the outsider, providing a view of the centre (the mainstream) that defamiliarizes habituated normalcy. The Fool indicts society by evoking a response from the community that belies the truth of their Christianity. The Fool is

free and so the world is disturbed by him; because he is useless and does not seek power … The fool bears witness to the basic discrepancy between human and divine wisdom. "Mocking" all forms of conventional morality based on rules, he affirms the cardinal worth of the person. As a little child, he points to the kingdom of heaven that is utterly different from every earthly kingdom. (20)

The person with a disability (especially if it involves mental illness or developmental disability) occupies space on the peripheries of social life together with the Holy Fool: dismissed, disdained as "useless" for not generating income, perceived as a lesser human (Garland Thomson, 148). The role of the Fool is to "show us what true sanity and wisdom are; they show us that we cannot absolutise the criteria of wholeness of life which this present world offers … Our humanity is a mystery which we are still exploring" (Saward, 52). The profound depth of our humanity is rooted in the person of Christ, the Incarnate One, and therefore cannot be measured through our typical empirical models. We can only effectively approach the fullness of our humanity through the Holy Trinity, which forces us to "revise our most fundamental ways of understanding reality. In particular, it makes us question our passive acceptance of the definition of sanity and madness, of wholeness and inadequacy, offered to us by our culture" (48).

As Christians committing to revitalizing our Christian faith, our sacred heritage powerfully demands a reappraisal of our treatment of those deemed "deviant" in our societies. We hear that our call reaches far beyond simple "accommodation" of those with disabilities and recognize that those judged as "other" or "special" are integral to the community of the Kingdom: the core to our being constituted as the people of God, as *ekklesia*. Just as the Fool stands "outside the Christian establishment" (Yannaras, cited in Saward, 31) so, too, those marked by disabilities call us to see our Christian community not as society constructs it, but as it is called to be eschatologically—in union with the Trinity. By rejecting those labelled disabled, inappropriate, or otherwise undesirable, the Christian community betrays its fundamental charism: to be a sign of the Kingdom in and for the world. Those who suggest that "there are places for people like that" other than "our place" fail to recognize the fullness of human community, the profound diversity of what constitutes true humanity, and the life of the Trinity to which we are called.

Holy Places of Interdependence

Ironically, the creation of "places" for those who are marginalized by society finds its origin in the history of Christianity. The first hospitals and similar institutions were creations of the Christian impulse to integrate all people into the community, whether one was wealthy or needy. Although pre-Christian societies had institutions akin to what we would regard as hospitals, it was Christianity that introduced an important shift in the development of the institution. The Christian impulse was for interdependence and community. Early Christian communities recognized a common responsibility not only for their members, but for all those who were in need. This determination matured within monastic settings, where it was understood that persons who were ill or infirm did not bear responsibility for their illness, but did require the assistance of others in order to return to health (Crislip, 76). Hence, from as early as Pachomius, we see monastic leaders aggressively calling fellow monastics to service and condemning any expression of stigmatization or shunning of the sick or disabled (Crislip, 89). This welcome of the needy comes to a powerful expression in the work of Basil the Great and his creation of Basileias or Basiliades—what we can easily recognize as a fourth-century hospital caring for the destitute, stranger, orphan, leper, sick, and elderly (Crislip, 101–16).

This complex of buildings was not just for monastics; it was at the heart of Basil's monastic city and addressed multiple medical and social needs. Its placement symbolically represented Basil's understanding of the sanctified social order as being built around the poor, not around the wealthy (Holman, 107). This eschatological social order, reflecting Trinitarian love, illuminates the justice that pervades the Gospel (109). Thus the *caritas* of Basil's community is based in respect, not pity, "combining personal respect with the supply of their necessity, and so giving them a double relief" (65). Instead of preaching on the plight of the poor, Basil and the Cappadocians demonstrate that the poor were not "outside the realm of civic obligations" (103).

Basil was concerned with challenging the exclusionary proclivities of the wealthy that limited their humanity and spiritual growth. He believed that the wealthy and those in need were interdependent and would benefit equally from each other. The wealthy manifest their spiritual conversion in extending assistance, whereas the sick, infirm, or homeless receive physical amelioration. Placing the one who is ill or in need at the centre of the community destabilizes the danger of complacency engendered by the comfort of wealth. In this way, Christian living involves instability and transformation; the Christian strives to be the agent of the transformative power of God's presence in the world. The Cappadocians "emphasized the universal nature of God's goodness to *all* creation. It is in these references to divine identity where we find the language of 'human rights' in the Gregories: terms referring explicitly to equality, rights, and freedom" (150). As a result, the poor are no longer "a passive tool for redemptive almsgiving" (54) but are powerful agents for social transformation.

Unfortunately, Basil's approach also unwittingly resulted in the demise of the transformative power of his model. Plainly intending to invigorate the community and spark a heightened sense of co-responsibility in being the Body of Christ, Basil addressed the equitable redistribution of wealth by directing alms "to those who can most wisely manage them" (111)— the bishops. Basil's desire to ensure just prosperity ultimately facilitated greater dichotomy by distancing the person with material affluence from the person without. This distance becomes both literal and figurative, enabling people on either pole to objectify the other. We cannot be "our brothers' [or sisters'] keeper" when we cannot recognize our brother and sister. Our responsibility shifts from being with and for other people to being for an institution or for a person in authority.

Geel: A Divine Sanctuary

Still, human response to perceived difference is not homogeneous, nor do human relationships follow a historical progression. In medieval Belgium, the town of Geel (Goldstein and Godemont) provides an example of Christian community where the presence of Christ's love creates divine sanctuary: the dwelling place of God who, as Trinity, is community. In the Middle Ages, the miraculous powers of a martyred Saint Dymphna became renowned in Europe. The oral tradition surrounding this seventh-century Irish martyr recounted the healing of mental illness.

The miracles arose from the place of her remains in Geel and involved a nine-day sojourn in the parish church. Because of the popularity of the site and the great numbers attending, the community of Geel chose to open its homes to those with mental illness who came in search of healing. Those who were healed would have been able to leave; however, the many who came and either waited their turn to access the church, or were not cured and stayed, needed lodging. In response, the parish clergy, in cooperation with the townspeople, organized billets for the visitors. The billeting quickly resulted in visitors remaining for extended periods of time or becoming permanent residents. Ultimately, the town became home for a disproportionately high population of people with mental illnesses. While the nature of these illnesses is unknown, the fact that people travelled distances in hope of cure and required care from the townsfolk suggests that we would consider their conditions disabilities. However, in Geel, in the town of welcome service and healing, mental illness was not a disability. Geel created the miracle of Christian community.

The image of Jesus the servant or the healer is of a person directly involved in the lives of others. The relationships are personal. They mirror the Trinitarian relationships and provide the template for true Christian community. They celebrate difference and recognize infirmity, illness, and disorder. They do not disable through demeaning attitudes. They heal through the miracle of love and make *caritas* the ethos of the community. They do not substitute mediated charity for intimate human connectedness. But they do threaten our sense of belonging to the norm, our sense of being like everyone else, our sense of complacency. Living the Trinitarian model confuses the border between me and we—our Western sense of being in control of our own lives and our own fate is placed in jeopardy. Can we feel comfortable in a community where a destabilizing diversity is at its core? Can we accept that we are strangers in a foreign land, or do we reject the premise and marginalize all those who remind us of our own strangeness? Do we reject those who are impaired because they place in relief our own inadequacies? "[M]any [Christians] are embarrassed because they cannot turn them into miracle fodder—for their disabilities are never healed" (Young, 97).

We were of course given holy water. We were encouraged to pray for a miracle. Others, too, prayed for the miracle. Yes, life would be easier if Aleksandra did not have Rett Syndrome. But is the Incarnation about life being easy? The miracle we really needed was for Aleksandra to come to know God through those around her. *We* are the ones who don't understand, who don't have the patience to be with her, to let her be who she is. *We* need healing. But do we want to be reminded of this fact in our daily lives?

8

Sacred Matter: Sacraments

I t may be disconcerting to admit uncertainty while focusing on our religious faith. Christianity seems to have had clearly delineated parameters: right is distinguished from its diametric opposite—wrong. Is not the line between human and divine, spiritual and material, even mind and body self-evident? Perhaps it seems odd to suggest that our Christian faith centres on ambiguity. And yet, despite our desire for the security that accompanies incontrovertible fact, Christianity rests on paradox: Jesus is both human and divine; God is three yet one; God saves by entering into the world, not removing us from it.

At its core, Christian faith is incarnational: we recognize God, get to know God, become like God in this world. Our faith affirms our situatedness and therefore affirms us as relational beings: we exist in relation to God, to each other, and to the cosmos. Thus our faith is rooted in our materiality, and this sacred substantiality, as it were, is manifested in sacramentality.

Creation Is Permeated with Divinity

Over the centuries, Christians have developed varying understandings of sacraments, but all reflect a basic insight: the holy works through the created. Whether we look at the origins of Christian Eucharist, discuss Luther's notion of salvation and grace, or engage in the contemporary debates over non-heterosexual marriage, we fundamentally question how the divine enters our human reality. While we do not claim to exhaustively answer the mystery, we believe that each and every Christian has a responsibility to be an agent of the divine—not in solitary acts, but as a member of the Body, the church community, in relationships that reflect the archetypal community of the Trinity. It is therefore the Church (as community) that is the primary place of meeting between divine and created. The Church is the first sacrament. In this way, we who claim the name of Christian are required to reflect the image of the Triune God.

The world is sacramental because it is the product of the divine creative act. Thus, in sustaining Christ's work of the Father, we are not Church just for ourselves, but for the world: God is with us *through us*. There is no other way we can know God except as we are embodied in the world. Our vocation as members of the Church is to transfigure the world into God's Kingdom: not by power and might, but by our witness and *caritas*. That is why we embrace each other's differences rather than producing deviance. Non-disabled and disabled alike celebrate that we are invited into the Trinitarian life, called to be holy, regardless of how "the world" sees us. This is life lived sacramentally.

Regulating the Sacred

Christians in the earliest period built on their Judaic tradition and recognized certain events in the life of the community as particularly intense moments of celebration of the divine presence. In the early Church (because of the dominance of Greek culture) these moments were called *mysterion*, or mysteries: not because they were secret, but because they were profound experiences that escaped full elucidation in words. The mysteries were events in which God's presence was most acutely experienced. In the Eastern churches, these mysteries have not been formally limited to any specific number, whereas in the medieval West, the desire for rational clarity and specificity resulted in delimiting the sacraments (from the Latin *sacramentum*) to seven. Although originally pointing to the intimate confluence of the divine and the created, eventually the promulgation of the idea of a binary opposition between spiritual and earthly resulted in the sacraments being understood as unique intrusions, so to speak, of the divine into the human. All too often, this view also led to an insistence on constructed understandings of human perfection as precursors of participation in the sacramental actions. A sacramental understanding of reality devolved into exclusive rituals demanding prerequisite conformity to socially acceptable norms. As a result, individuals with various disabilities have been denied participation or judged as "not needing the sacrament." We must recover the fuller understanding of the world's sacramentality and apply it to our community's understanding of its sacraments.

The Sacraments of Initiation

Since the 1960s, Christian churches have undergone a communal rediscovery of the rites of Christian initiation: Baptism and Eucharist, as well as Chrismation/Confirmation for some. This process was led by the Faith and Order Commission of the World Council of Churches and resulted in the Lima Document of 1982, entitled *Baptism, Eucharist, and Ministry*. Most Christian churches continue to agree that Baptism with a Trinitarian formula is normative for entry into the community. However, although at times nuanced, that entry is completed not in the baptismal act, but in joining the community at the table: the Eucharist. These two moments are common and clearly defined. Historically, there was also a third moment: an anointing with a specific oil, (usually) called "chrism." This third moment gradually has changed in some traditions, in both nomenclature and timing. Baptism marked a recognition of Jesus as Saviour and incorporation into the mystery of his death and Resurrection. Chrismation marked the individual as a member of the Body and so a recipient and bearer of the Holy Spirit. Being brought to the eucharistic table signalled full entry into the community—that is, full entry into the divine life (as already, but not yet). In short, the person is initiated into a set of interconnected, but salvific, relationships. Corporately, the Christian community marked and celebrated new members who were recognizing and joining the Church as the pre-eminent body through which they would come to meet and know God.

In the first five centuries of Christianity, it was normative for the candidate for community membership to be baptized, chrismated, and then brought to Eucharist. Eventually, in Western Christianity, the act of anointing (Chrismation) came to be called Confirmation. Because, in the West, Confirmation required the ministry of a bishop, in the fifth and sixth centuries it was postponed for years when necessary, until the bishop could be accessed. Eventually, the rite was moved from being between the other two moments to stand alone, often long after the person was receiving Eucharist. Confirmation came to be regarded as an individual's acceptance of Baptism, although theologically, the notion of "accepting" the grace of Baptism is problematic. Once demonstration of intellectual assent was required in order to receive the sacrament, the possibility arose that people with developmental disabilities or severe physical restrictions to communication could be forbidden to take part. During the Reformation, some Christian churches abandoned Confirmation entirely. Whether encouraging or dismissing Confirmation, it was common to understand the action as one between the individual and God, not reflecting community relationships.

Intellect versus Experience

Questions of intellectual assent or verbal acceptance of "a sacrament" also entered into Christian debates over Baptism. Although adult baptism, marking a profound conversion, was the dominant form of initiation for centuries, evidence for infant baptism suggests that it, too, has apostolic roots. Some scholars point to Acts 16:14-15, the baptism of Lydia's household, presumably including children, as implicit evidence for infant baptism. Tertullian's (c. 160–c. 220) opposition to infant baptism verifies the existence of the practice ("On Baptism", 678). In considering the treatment of people with intellectual disabilities, the arguments for and against infant baptism are significant, because they raise the question of understanding, or the ability to demonstrate understanding. Similarly, part of the rationale for observing Confirmation when a child can "know right from wrong" relates to the very same question of comprehension.

This increasing emphasis on intellectual consent mirrored the West's growing regard for rationality and the autonomous individual. During the Reformation, radical reformers such as Menno Simons (1496–1561) and Conrad Grebel (c. 1498–1526) insisted that Baptism could only follow an adult's individual declaration of faith. Ironically, despite Luther's dismissal of people who are not in control of their bodies (see the earlier discussion of the changeling of Desau), he also denounces the argument of those for whom demonstrable reasoning is imperative for Baptism. Luther emphatically insists that "reason in no way contributes to faith" (Luther, 353). Nonetheless, the persistence of infant baptism indicates that Christians, at least implicitly, have regarded faith as gift—to be received with no contingencies of understanding—at the moment of Baptism. The communities that continue the practice of infant baptism demonstrate their commitment to witness the faith to that person so she or he may grow in the experience of God's presence in her or his life. Faith is preserved as a communal experience, not simply a matter of intellectual assent.

In some traditions, most particularly those of the Eastern churches, this same logic is extended to the rites of Chrismation and Eucharist (which still retain their original order). In these churches, an infant will receive all three sacraments within one liturgical experience. That infant is not expected to "understand" the event; rather, she or he is received into the community on the faith of her or his parents (and godparents), and it is assumed that the infant will grow within the community to experience fully a life with Christ. The infant is initiated into a web of relationships, all of which serve one purpose: to come to know God in one's own capacity. Within such a paradigm, no "special" place is required for the person with an intellectual impairment. She or he is an integral member of the community from birth and will continue to be so until death.

Christian traditions that have shifted from this model continue to grapple with the issues surrounding judgments of an individual's understanding of the meaning of the rites of initiation, which often results in the prohibition of persons with intellectual disabilities from full participation in the life of the Church. This exclusion invariably inflicts additional grief, not only on the individual, but also on his or her family and friends. Another common form of ostensible accommodation, arising from good intentions, is the practice of worship services for designated groups. Although these are an attempt to include groups that are habitually overlooked in the larger assembly, rather than adjusting the larger assembly's practice, these "special" liturgies perpetuate marginalization. Since Christian worship, liturgy, is widely regarded as marking the life of the Church in its fullness (Schmemann, 12), we must remember that centuries of Christian practice persistently attest that liturgy is for the entire Body. Worship is meant to be an inclusive act of the community that binds all members together and is in no way regulated by ability. Worship constitutes the Church and creates sanctuary.

So, where do we Christians belong? Or more to the point, to what community do we want to belong? We are in the world, but are we of the world? The world devalues Aleksandra: she will not work (generate income), vote (fulfill a civic duty), feed herself (experience autonomy). The world's standards say she is a burden on society. But what about the Church? Will Aleksandra know acceptance for who she is? Will there be a community of respect and support when we, her parents, die? Or will she become invisible because she is a failed miracle?

9

Mad About Miracles

There is no doubt about it; we are mad about miracles. Miracles make headlines. Miracles inspire. We long for them, need them, pray for them, sing about them, read about them, watch movies about them. If nothing else, we laugh about them: What a miracle; the train is on time! Miracles are definitely crowd pleasers. Miracles entertain and delight, like magic shows or circus wonders.

On the other hand, in modern society we also are ambivalent towards miracles, scorning any phenomena that lack a scientific explanation even as lucrative industries around "the supernatural" metamorphose into fashionable forms palatable to current tastes. Fortune telling, aura reading, and angel talk attest to people's need for a reality existing beyond the scientific gold standard of empirical proof. Ostensibly, miracles inspire belief in God; or, when they don't happen as requested or expected, they destroy faith: easy come, easy go! In some ways, miracle requests reveal our need for God as an insurance policy. We tend to rely on ourselves, on our independence, intelligence, hard work, or what have you, until our strengths run out. Then we remember the God policy and file for a miracle claim to regain our self-reliance.

Miracles may be lots of things to lots of people, but if you have a disability, miracles are not something you can ignore as much as you may want. When you are labelled "disabled," the concept of miracles as an instantaneous fixing of presumed brokenness clings to you like chewing gum in tangled hair. And this is what makes us, as parents of our daughters, really mad about miracles. Miracles, as they are popularly known and as they are piously regarded in the Christian Church, cause harm. Miracles and the sensational industry generated by them play a significant role in disabling people—alienating them from the mainstream and keeping them in the margins of society and faith communities.

A quick fix to a problem is enticing. The latest "miracle" drug or food or potion never seems to lack a dedicated discipleship, whether it purports to cure cancer or melt away unwanted pounds. Time and again, when people encountered our children, the notion of miracle would arise, together with the assurance that God is good. It clearly baffled people that a priest whom they loved and respected would be "stricken" so "tragically" with disability in the family. We were told in no uncertain terms that our first daughter (only days old and struggling to survive) was born so that our church community could witness a miracle. As she grew, we had to learn not to react negatively to kindly, incessant advice to take her to Lourdes, Fatima, and countless other sites known for their miracle cures. Once our youngest daughter manifested the effects of a degenerative condition, it became commonplace to be given gifts (on loan or to keep) of saint's relics, holy water, holy oil, and even holy sand from places of reputable miracle fame. While ever grateful to our friends and parishioners for the kindness of their intent, as our family grew older we became acutely aware of the insidious degradation that these kindnesses engendered, within the larger context of our experience.

Does this sound harsh?

We have written earlier in this book about the disabling of people by social structures and by attitudes that ultimately demean others under the guise of charity and goodwill. The notion of society creating disability can be a difficult idea to recognize, just as the idea that language or discourse (as the specific repetitive use of a language in a given context) creates reality. We have also touched on how acknowledging disability's social construction should not overlook corporeal experience. Although matter is not created by discourse, it is interpreted and given meaning through discourse.

I have my body, but how I understand its function and value depends on the interplay between the personal context I was born into, including my genetic inheritance, and my social, cultural, and political contexts and relationships. These contexts create a familiar but limiting language that forms concepts into words and uses words to form concepts that are then received as "common" knowledge. The discourse of disability as deviance includes the discourse of miracles. This "common" language includes ideas of people with disabilities as a problem, but includes no words to shape ideas of people with disabilities as anything else: problem/abnormal or not problem/normal. These processes, through which society shapes unconventional bodies as defective, emphasize the constructed nature of everyone's reality. The artificial dualism of the normal/abnormal binary prevents us in either category from engaging the fullness of our humanity.

In our experience as parents, learning about the theoretical concept of society manufacturing deviance, or defect, and how discourse embeds this product into our collective understanding so that we believe it is natural fact, shed light on the daily discriminatory practices surrounding disability that our family encountered.

We were and are constantly appalled by the absence of popular outrage in the face of the systemic and personalized bigotry against disability. Similar treatment targeting women or visible minorities has surely provoked protest. How could we articulate the critical fact that our children were not the burden we were told they were? The way most people and all social institutions treated our family frequently drove us to despair, and yet these very people and systems attributed any and all hardship to our children first, and then to us. Ostensibly, our children were obliged to act as if they were not "disabled," and we were obliged to function as if they were not disabled. If we failed at this social task, we were at risk of being categorized as "needy" and dysfunctional. Actually, proof of this type of failure was requisite to being eligible for most "disability services."

How are we to interpret our daughter's place in the world when every image in her books that describes a body somehow similar to hers characterizes a tragic, pathetic, or unwanted individual? How was she to respond to her Grade 10 class study of *The Miracle Worker*, named for the teacher, Anne Sullivan, who tames the wild, animalistic Helen Keller and forces her into the human species by making her speak? The upshot of the story implies that those who cannot speak are simply failed humans. Likewise, a parishioner assured us that if a person with a disability has understanding, then she or he will inevitably find a way to let others know, no matter how severe the impairment. This view exemplifies the persistence of a mind/body dichotomy that presumes superiority of mind over body. Unintentionally, our parishioner has condemned to non-intelligence all individuals who have no way to communicate their subjectivity. Those whose minds cannot control their bodies are in effect judged to have no mind, hence justifying infantilized treatment (recall Luther's extreme conclusion to this sentiment). Just as society has not created space or language in our mainstream understanding for the value of a citizen when her body is severely "impaired," so, too, our faith communities have fallen short of fulfilling our Christian calling by following these social norms of exclusion. Disability erodes the security sought in our hallowed mythologies of personal control and independence. Focusing on the questions that disability poses in our church communities forces us to confront our perspectives on what "we" means. Who is "different" and why? Focusing on disability as Christians forces us to acknowledge who constitutes the "other" for us and exhorts us to continually seek out and bring in the other. Living the Trinitarian faith recognizes an "other" as a continual extension of self (myself or ourselves). This recognition produces respect and awe for the relationship that once again "continually" revitalizes the sanctuary that is community.

Our eldest daughter did not know she was "disabled" until she was in Grade 4. Until that time she was chronically ill, she used a wheelchair, she could not straighten her arms, and she experienced periods of extreme pain. At the same time, in her home environment, she was able to get around anywhere she wanted in any way she could. She was the elder sister of two adoring siblings; she went to dance classes, sang in a choir, cooked meals with the family, and so on. In other words, her body was as it was and she did what she could with and in, not despite, her body. If her body was "different" from mine, for example, it was not "abnormal"; it was very normally hers.

We are not idealizing the home pole of the inside/outside binary presented here. The "outside" discrimination greeted us daily and eroded our well-being as parents. Happily, our daughter was too busy staying alive, with extremely precarious health, to notice how people treated her. If she was excluded, we were excluded as a family, so the impact on her, as a small child, was not obvious. Perhaps because she was our first child, together with the knowledge that she was not expected to survive her premature birth, we were extraordinarily grateful for and proud of her survival. Because medical specialists predicted her death, her life became a "miracle" as defined in the dictionary: "a remarkable and very welcome occurrence" (Oxford, 574).

While others expected a miraculous cure for her, for us the miracle was our child's tenacity at breathing when we knew we might lose her at any time. Physical impairment paled next to imminent death. At home, our daughter's body was extraordinary—miraculous. She was unable to walk, but she could bend her limbs in directions no one else could. She delighted us as she discovered unpredictable ways to move in her environment. If it seems unlikely, it is nonetheless true that she did not feel hampered or devalued for being as she was. Contrary to many people's presumption, the question "Why me?" was not a preoccupation for our daughter and, therefore, not for us. Living with her illustrated the disjuncture between what a non-disabled mainstream presumes is self-evident about disability and the experience of living in an unconventional body.

In Grade 4, however, the teacher saw our eldest as the "special needs" student and treated her as a pariah. Eventually, students followed suit. It was a devastating—indeed, crippling—experience for our daughter. Her body at home was clever, flexible, exciting in its extraordinary angles and curves. Her body at school was deformed, deviant. The home environment brought into relief the profound depth of social inscriptions on a person's reality.

Our schools were Catholic, our communities Christian, yet our family more often than not struggled with the façade of normalcy (act as if we have slept at night; don't make others uncomfortable; smile and nod) or struggled with the injustice of being relegated to the stage of specialness and charitable pity.

In our household, "special" came to be used sarcastically, as a pejorative. When we first heard the term "special" used to signify our child, we imagined the speaker could have easily substituted the label of "leper." We have found that the "special" label satisfies many people's need to distance themselves from the disabled individual while feeling kind and virtuous. And yet, many parents of children with disabilities do find comfort in the "special" label, probably because it is, at least superficially, positive in what often seems to be a hostile world. Nevertheless, in reference to disability, the use of "special" generally euphemistically denotes a subordinate or adapted event or thing. Simi Linton argues that the term characterizes a Freudian "reaction formation ... the unconscious defense mechanism in which an individual adapts attitudes and behaviours that are opposite to his or her own true feelings, in order to protect the ego from the anxiety felt from experiencing the real feelings" (16).

When our third daughter was diagnosed with Rett Syndrome as a toddler, our world changed. There is no space in this book to describe the planet onto which these events transported us as a family, but we would like to note the process of Othering that accompanied the shift from our position as a family with a child with a physical disability to a family who had a child with a developmental disability. Whereas our eldest daughter's capabilities and articulateness underlined the attitudinal exclusion of people with disabilities from our society through inaccessible built environments, our youngest child's loss of language and body control revealed a systemic exclusion that spelled something more chilling: a rejection of the perceived Other from the human category. Her body relegated her to an entirely separate standard of treatment that would be unthinkable for the "average" person. Her experience, and ours as her family, are immersed so thoroughly in a narrative of abnormality that it borders on the impossible to envision an alternate text.

A multilayered discourse of monstrosity permeates the environment around those labelled "severely disabled," justifying their alienation and subhuman treatment. Care for our youngest child's needs is characterized necessarily as a hardship, both social and personal. Even after decades of policies of deinstitutionalization, professional systems and popular opinion urge parents to "put away" their "defective" offspring, seemingly for the good of the family and the child involved. If "kept" at home, the situation is deemed successful only if the family presents a normal façade, erasing traces of dis/ease for those around them, carrying on with schedules of work and recreation as expected. Failure to do so marks a failed family, failed parents, an inability to cope—a family destroyed by the burden of "dependency." What does someone hear when she or he receives frequent invitations to healing services or pilgrimages to shrines, but never is invited to a birthday party or sleepover? What do we do to someone when we want her to be different from who she is? We want a miracle to change her. The difference of disability is most often permanent. How do I feel knowing that those around me wish I were not ... me?

The fact is that our child has done nothing to deliberately occasion her prohibition from community relationship. The real "burden" for our family is not our daughter but the systematized social arrangements that refuse to value her as a human being. The grief generated by our ongoing struggles with the educational and health systems that mistreat our daughter is matched by the effect of non-disabled people habitually relating to her as either a pariah or a pet gerbil. At home with her parents and sisters, with some close friends, our youngest is able to be as she is. Her lack of control over bodily functions is not embarrassing; her drooling is neither shocking nor repulsive. She is wholly unknowable in her unusual body with its deteriorating systems, yet, at the same time, she is simply one of us. When a number of people respond to her with the care she requires, no one needs to be overworked or deprived of other pursuits.

This idea of cooperative care is activated in Jean Vanier's L'Arche communities, established for and with people with disabilities. In his vision, these homes are meant to be places of openness, welcome, struggle, and growth. Vanier's hope is that here, where "we are accepted with our limitations as well as our abilities, community gradually becomes a place of liberation. Discovering that we are accepted and loved by others, we are better able to accept and love ourselves" (Vanier, 2). However, these "homes" are "special" indeed: although there are 137 homes in 40 countries around the world, there can never be enough, and they hover on the threshold of institutional care. Many of the care-giving members come and go instead of sharing a relatively permanent home with the residents.

Presumably, if we lived in a society or community that accepted and valued the unpredictable variety of human embodiment, more people would want to understand and appreciate our youngest daughter's unique way of being. The experience of the city of Geel, described in Chapter 7, attests to this hope. More people would want to be with Aleksandra, to be her friend. People might honestly want to get to know her, not just to be charitable or to fulfill a project requirement in social work. Imagine … if we lived as committed Christians, all people could experience the joy of affirmation as a valued member of Christ's body—family—Trinity. We would create the holy space. We would create sanctuary. We would experience miracle.

Given the weight Jesus' miracles have sustained throughout generations, and the insidious burden miracles have placed on people labelled "disabled," we want to simply, briefly, illustrate the problem of miracles from our current experience of disability and the Christian Church. Why should we all be mad about miracles? Why should we be mad about the way pious notions of miracles serve to oppress the very people Jesus demonstrated were central to the Kingdom of God, the Kingdom that he as the incarnate God proclaimed as present in the world? First, let us review some of the presuppositions that surround what is in essence the cult of miracle.

Miracles are associated with faith, sin, cure, prayer, and the power of God over nature to perform the impossible—even bring the dead back to life. In our time, we have created disability as deviance rather than understanding it as an ordinary human occurrence. We distance people with disabilities in our collective psyche as individual victims of misfortune. Unable (or unwilling) to relate to their experience, we tend to recoil and expect that the disabling condition be erased, either from existence or from our sight. A miracle presents a quick fix, a solution that demands nothing from us as fellow human beings. As much as it belies Christ's message, popular impressions persist in linking sin and disability, even if not consciously. It is not uncommon to hear sentiments such as "Why would he deserve such punishment?" "Why would God make her suffer so; what has she done?" Often, mainstream parish communities imagine a disabled parishioner (or his or her family) is targeted for particular trials by God—an unenviable position, to say the least.

Then there is typically the plea for a removal of the plight. This is not to say that prayer in any form is wrong, but rather that prayer is directed at rendering the disabled individual as not disabled. (We must keep in mind that situations vary, and in this general overview, the disability as such may or may not entail suffering beyond that imposed by bias and prejudice.) When the expected cure fails to occur, the marked person is further blamed (not necessarily overtly) for the failure: too little faith, too little prayer, too much of a sinner. Not only does the disability persist, but he or she has disappointed the community by not being miraculously cured. In short, the expectation of miracles stigmatizes and devalues individuals as insufficient; the lack of divine interception to restore them to an acceptable normalcy suggests alienation by God as well.

There is also the problem of the biblical miracle accounts themselves, which seem to tell us that faith in Christ's power to heal will be rewarded. If Jesus was moved with compassion to heal someone with epilepsy 2,000 years ago, why would he not heal my child's epilepsy? Why is my faith inadequate? Is Christ's compassion so arbitrary? Why should it be necessary to travel to Lourdes, for example, to seek a miracle, when we regularly take part in the Eucharist and the sacraments? Is some holiness more holy than others? Just thinking about miracles can be maddening!

Of course there is nothing wrong with desiring a cure for our problems, whatever they may be. Jesus performed miracles that cured people, among other wonders such as walking on water and saving a party by turning water into a good wine. Too often, the miracle narratives are presumed to provide proof that Jesus was God. However, biblical scholarship rejects this idea. Raymond Brown argues that in the Gospel accounts, Jesus himself puts little stock in the response to miracles: "If someone should rise from the dead, they would not be convinced" (Luke 16:31) (171). Contemporary miracle workers were not unusual among pagans and Hebrews alike. Jesus differentiated himself from other wonder workers by eschewing spectacle, not taking money, not punishing, and not performing on request. "Whether the request came from the devil, Herod, the Pharisees, or the people, Jesus would not perform miracles just to show that he was sent by God" (171). Disability Studies has criticized a common Christian correlation of sin with disability and the negative effects of Gospel cures that equate wholeness with redemption. Again, while these notions may be prevalent on a popular level, they are not validated by biblical exegesis. When studied as a whole, there is an absence of cause and effect in the miracle narratives. Miracles have occurred between Jesus and people of great faith or weak faith or no faith at all (Bornkamm et al., 282–83).

What can be the meaning of all those miracle stories?

Perhaps one of the most significant aspects of the miracle stories is that they are indeed stories. They follow a typical pattern for miracle accounts and, like any narrative, they are open to interpretation. The stories are recounted not to record historical data, but to emphasize a teaching about or of Christ. Over time, the theological lessons understood from the miracle events have varied in emphasis. Much energy has been spent in attempting to assess the events scientifically or to verify their occurrence in time. Walter Kasper submits that the miracle stories should be described as legends and we should accept them "as statements of faith about the significance for salvation of the person and message of Jesus" (90). Kasper explains why it would be futile to search for literal truth in the details of miracle narratives. For instance,

> Literary criticism reveals a tendency to intensify, magnify and multiply the miracles. According to Mk 1.34, Jesus healed many sick; in the parallel Mt 8.16 he heals them all. In Mark Jairus's daughter is on the point of death; in Matthew she is already dead. The healing of one blind man and one possessed becomes the healing of two blind men and two possessed. The feeding of the 4000 becomes the feeding of the 5000, and the seven baskets left over become twelve. If this tendency to develop, multiply and intensify can be found in the gospels themselves, then naturally it must also be presumed to have existed in the period before our gospels were compiled. This reduces the material on which the miracle reports are based very considerably. (89)

While critical biblical scholarship agrees that Jesus' actions made a powerful impression on those around him, the evangelists would have had to acknowledge his wonder working in order to establish his authority as a leader. Emphasizing the miracles of Jesus further illuminates Christ as the one who fulfills the prophecies of Isaiah. Despite the popular attention given to the details of healing narratives, determining who was healed and why, the more significant aspect of these events appears to be not the act of physical curing, but rather that the miracles were performed on the Sabbath, flaunting the norms of the mainstream religious establishment (Brown, 174; Kasper, 90).

When rereading the miracle narratives within the Trinitarian paradigm of relationship that we are tracing through sacred history in this volume, Christ's embodiment of Trinity is reinforced. The miraculous actions of Jesus do not simply transgress the codified rules of his day; his miracles, regardless of actual details, transcend entrenched inequality and bias. The prevailing message manifested by the miracle stories is the presence of the Kingdom of God—not by Jesus' performance of supernatural wonders, but by his refusal to allow social constructions of human worth to obstruct the sacred power of relationship. The miracle accounts reveal that the Incarnation was not to perfect a broken world, but rather to demonstrate that the brokenness is perfected in love. Jesus reached out to others, interacted with them, engaged in conversation with them, and responded to them as equal human beings, whether it was a day that prohibited response or whether their stigma prohibited interaction. This is the message of the miracles that we see crystallizing in their summary and that has become severely distorted through subsequent ages into our day. Jesus in fact did not heal "the lame," the "blind," or "the woman's bleeding." Jesus healed individuals whom he met, spoke to, touched in some way. He did not end disability or eradicate leprosy or cure cancer. Rather, by his example, he eradicated the shame that accompanied those shunned by society for being as they are—ill, impaired, ugly, woman, child, tax collector, poor, non-Jew, and so on.

Jesus lived *caritas*. He created a living sanctuary here on earth where all humanity, all matter, is divinized as we participate in the relationship of the Trinity. Raymond Brown notes the difference in the vocabulary of miracles in the Johannine accounts. The term "sign," referring to Jesus' miraculous deeds by others, is differentiated from the term "work," used specifically by Jesus (according to exegetes) to refer to his miracles (Brown, 181). Jesus does not refer to his miracles as signs and, as mentioned above, scorns the need for them. The significance is staggering when we consider that the term "work" is also used for Jesus' entire ministry, referring to the Father's mission, which implies a heritage of God's work throughout history. Also, "work" is correlated to "word" (181–82, fn 45), further establishing that the miracle works of Jesus demonstrate the presence of God *in the same way* that his life manifests the Father.

In this aspect, the details of the miracles themselves become irrelevant, except in that they illuminate the dignity of the individuals who engage with Jesus and with whom Jesus engages. When the miracles of Jesus are recognized as his *works*, they essentially disengage from the magical quality that Jesus rejected. Jesus' life and works proclaimed the Kingdom (God's presence) here and now—not as an occasional miraculous appearance, but as present in the fullness of humanity. The miracle is not a product of the unnatural, but rather an event of the natural world, because Jesus is fully human and fully God.[12] The miracle is the Incarnation and the recognition of our participation in it.

Living as Trinity, we, too, create miracles in our relationships with one another, rejecting social hierarchies and enveloping each other in love. We are all invited to be active miracle workers, not by invoking the deity to act, but rather by allowing the Holy Spirit to transfigure us into the People of God, into community, into sanctuary.

In developed societies, social service agencies are supposed to exist to support families. A typical service is respite provision, whereby a worker comes into the family home to perform care-giving duties to give the caregiver a break. The concept is commendable; however, the more intense and unusual the needed care, the less likely it is that you will find an adequate worker. What is more, it is often not easy to access respite services, which have waiting lists that render the notion of service ludicrous. In our region, at the time of writing, most in-home services have a waiting list of one to two years. We know a family that has been waiting for four years now. If a family member requires constant care, while parents are expected to pursue careers, either extended family networks must be activated in full force or the expected framework collapses. The cared-for person, under these circumstances, becomes the source of problems: ruined career, income loss, burnout, the need for "charity." The logical solution to this dilemma justifies the removal of the problem to an institutional milieu that will control and manage the disturbance so that normalcy can be restored. The unforgivable sin in this societal event is that the family has failed to pretend to be "normal"; the child with disabilities has failed to disappear within family management. Societal systems dehumanize the profoundly human realities of disability. As Christians, do we want to know charity or *caritas*? Do we perceive problems or people?

---

12 See Kasper on the untenability of explaining miracles as unnatural acts of God (91–92).

10

Sanctuary: Abnormal Hospitality

O ur parishes are most frequently associated with a physical building—a church, a sanctuary. When we hear the word "sanctuary,"
we may think of a holy place or a refuge where people have sought
safety from punishment or legal action. The practice of claiming sanctuary,
as in current Canadian examples where individuals reside in a church to
avoid deportation, draws on the ancient pre-Christian belief that "normal"
rules do not apply to sacred spaces. A place becomes sacred because it is
the dwelling place of God. In the presence of the deity, society's laws have
no relevance.

We enter the sanctuary to be sanctified. For the first Christians, the
Incarnation shifted the understanding of sanctuary from place to people.
"For where two or three are gathered in my name, I am there among them"
(Mt. 18:20). Christ *is* present for the Christian communities. Sheldrake,
in *Spaces for the Sacred,* explains how the early church communities perceived themselves as God's dwelling place and, therefore, lent sanctity to
the places they inhabited.

> The locus of the sacred transgresses former boundaries and is to
> be found particularly where people seek to be a community in
> Christ, distinguished by the destruction of traditional separations
> and by a quality of common life. Christ is to be met in those who

are rejected or excluded in the old religious and cultural dispensation—the hungry, thirsty, naked, imprisoned, women, Samaritans, Romans, publicans, sinners. (Mt. 1.23; 25.31ff.) (37–38)

When we recognize the profound impact the life of Jesus had on the faith traditions of those who immediately followed him, and when we try to trace that impact to our present time, a few elements crystallize as imperative to the desire to be Christian. Certainly followers of Christ would necessarily be distinguishable from non-followers in that they function as living sanctuary, fully conscious and glad of human interdependence. Followers of Christ would be impelled to create community—collective—since an embrace of our humanness demands acknowledgement of our need for others in whatever capacity. (To be human is to be needy. Self-sufficiency is an artificial contingent notion. A most able-bodied resourceful individual would not survive without initial nurturing from others.)

As Christians, we would have no choice but to reject the exclusions of mainstream normalcy, while making the spaces we inhabit holy, encompassing our humanity and meeting the humanity of others, most specifically those who are pushed to the peripheries of power. To be Christian we must be Trinity. In the sanctuary of the Trinity, knowing that we need each other—our incapacities, inadequacies, frailties, impairments, even our pain and suffering—is a fact of our being and is gladly accommodated as much as possible. Caring *about* naturally includes caring *for* each other. Caring *for* would not be burdensome, because it would be shared, and we would be grateful to a receiver of care for giving us the joy of being of service to him or her. In the sanctuary of authentic Christian community, we would be respected and loved as fellow Christians with, not despite, our limitations. In this sense, in the Christian sanctuary, where society's norms become irrelevant in the sacred presence of the triune God, no one is disabled.

Sound utopian? Unrealistic? Impossible? This paradigm of Christian community requires a deep commitment of persons to desire and seek to accept their humanity, to unlearn a value system that places income generation as a prerequisite for social worth and participation. Yet this Christian community is no more impossible than it would be for a group of people to enjoy Jesus' example of inclusion so much that non-Christians would document their astonishment at the joy and love they witnessed. Tertullian (c. 160–c. 220) reports that when Roman pagans saw Christian communities, they marvelled at "how they love one another" (39:7). But this image of love and service is not one that is limited to some long ago era. The example of the community of Geel, Belgium, continues to this day. The townspeople of Geel continue to be the miracle initiated in medieval Christianity.

> If a stigma related to mental illness exists at all in Geel, it is a positive stigma. The presence of patients in town life is so common that they are welcomed and even nurtured by the entire community. At one and the same time, the citizens of Geel accept those with mental illness *and* the fact that they are members of the community. (Goldstein and Godemont, 442)

Over its long history, the community of Geel has become a welcoming, inclusive town that does not regard itself as exceptional; being sanctuary is the norm. This is mirrored in the (previously related) experience of deaf people on Martha's Vineyard in the nineteenth century, when the extent of deafness meant that sign language was a common mode of communication even for hearing residents (Groce). Although these examples continue to be exceptional, they need not be.

> What Geel does, simply because they are used to doing it, can be done by any community—with motivation, education, and effort. What Geel has always done and still does today is: (a) acknowledge and accept the human needs of the boarders and (b) respond to those needs rather than acting on unfounded or exaggerated fears. (Goldstein and Godemont, 456)

Focusing on the elision of disability from the "normal" consciousness of our contemporary parishes can bring into relief the tradition of Christian faith that has steadfastly reflected on the meaning of Christ's teaching and sustained his radical call to recognize and realize our intrinsic interconnectedness. What is required, then, is conversion to a new, Trinitarian understanding of human community.

Our family, unwittingly, entered a whole new world: the world of disability. We knew little of this world until we found ourselves there—in a parallel existence with a distinct view of the normal world while being bizarrely invisible to it. In the (dis) world we have met people from all sectors of society, all cultures, all colours … There seems to be a consensus; everyone dreams of a miracle. The miracle would be a world in which our differences would make no difference. And so our differences would be valued facets of our valued lives.

11

Transfigured Corporeality:
Being Icons

With the fall of the Soviet Union and the subsequent struggle of Eastern European countries to rediscover former faith traditions, there has been a resurgence in both academic and popular interest in Eastern Christian iconography. Under communist rule, the ancient iconographic practice of visual prayer was officially suppressed; icons were generally relegated to the museums, displayed as cultural art, emptied of spiritual significance. A theological focus on disability within our Christian tradition illuminates the significance of iconography in our everyday lives.

Iconography asserts corporeal reality in all its frailty, vulnerability, and dependence as the mandatory experience for salvation. By reflecting on the popular icons of the Trinity, Nativity, and Resurrection, we see boundaries dissolve. The dissolution of boundaries between the perceived dichotomies of mind and body, the sacred and carnal, as well as theory and experience, reveal embodiment rather than ability as the prerequisite for human fulfilment.

The work of scholars who have theorized from their own subjective experience of disability and pain suggests that the heightened awareness of corporeality that disability entails leads to an experience of transcendence that belies the Cartesian dualism of mind/body that dominates Western thinking.[13] The very notion of transcendence usually connotes a negation of body, a state of being beyond flesh, presumably higher, purer, cerebral. We use the language of disembodiment, otherworldliness, supernatural. However, experiences such as those described by the philosopher Susan Wendell discover a transcendence that is possible to achieve only through an acute consciousness of body that she acquired once disabled. She is one of many who encounter a consciousness beyond body, through body. Evidently, there is more to us than body and mind, but our dualistic language patterns hinder a negotiation around the vertiginous interplay of factors comprising embodied identity.

Rather than having a sense of alienation from her body, Wendell describes bodily transcendence as an "increase of freedom" that "expands the possibilities of experience beyond the miseries and limitations of the body" (178). Freedom from the oppression her chronic pain imposes stems from intimate knowledge of her body, rather than a rejection of it. Transcending the negative in one's body is not an "out of body" experience. Instead, it is the heightened understanding of one's corporeal self that has led to a deeper awareness of the possibilities of self—of consciousness—of being. Without body, consciousness as we know it does not exist.

Bodily transcendence, then, does not negate body but finds autonomy from what seem to be overwhelming goings-on in the body. A new understanding of our physical self can uncover formerly unrecognized realities of consciousness. Wendell describes how her "body led [her] to a changed identity, to a very different sense of [her]self …" (175). Precisely because she is living with a disability, Wendell is less affected by physical vicissitudes than when she was well. In this way, "independence" from some of our body's troubles can be understood as an interdependence of the complex that constitutes self. The reduction of being into two separate and distinct categories is as much a socio-cultural construct as the myth of individual independence so privileged by Western culture (144–51). We in the West deride the notion of "dependency." People receiving social assistance, as well as people with visible disabilities, are perceived as needy—dependent—while the pervasive reliance on cars, telephones, electricity, and

---

13 For example, see the works of Eisland, Murphy, and Wendell.

buildings is not conceived as a dependency. Yet, just as independence—complete non-reliance on other human beings—isn't possible, neither body nor mind is independent of the other.

Privileging mind over body overlooks the fact that mind does not have complete power and control over matter and, on the other hand, that people do not exist as bodies without minds. Too often, because of a dysfunctional body that prevents conventional modes of speech, a person is perceived as mindless because we as a society refuse to acknowledge that which we do not understand. Wendell's experience of transcendence can shatter the conceptual obstruction constructed between mind and body by manifesting a human ability to exert not mind over matter, but matter into consciousness.

Despite Christ's embrace of human lived reality, current popular culture associates Christianity with vilifying flesh as the vehicle for sin. Images abound of medieval women and men mortifying their bodies with self-flagellation and hair shirts. Indeed, a strain of body derogation has continued throughout Western Christian history. As recently as the mid-20th century, the Roman Catholic Church proclaimed the doctrine of the Assumption of Mary. Her bodily ascension into heaven asserts not the value of her human body, but rather its sinlessness and thus its extraordinary, un-body-like conclusion. Venerated in the Roman Church as the immaculately conceived Blessed Virgin Mary, handmaid and Mother of God, her special status derives from what for most of us would be a very unrecognizable life experience.

In contrast, the Christian churches of the East commemorate this event—the end of the Mother of God's existence on earth—as the Dormition: the falling asleep. She is honoured as first among saints (historical individuals). Her sanctified life and critical role in sacred history culminate in an ordinary but angst-free end. The Christian East maintains a deeply incarnational theology. Rather than highlight humanity's fallen state, the Eastern Christian Church has largely sustained its focus on the mystery of embodied divinity and the radical ramifications of this event in history. The fourth-century Athanasius of Alexandria's assertion that God "indeed assumed humanity that we might become God" (54) is central to Eastern Christian incarnational theology and underpins the tradition of iconography. Every Eastern Christian, regardless of occupation, class, or gender, is called to reflect Christ in her or his life, to be an icon of Christ. Supported by the annual church cycle of prescribed liturgical and sacramental ritual, an individual strives towards divinization[14] by seeking to be authentically human. Like Wendell's progress through matter into consciousness, through embodiment the Eastern Christian discovers Christ.

This practice of visual theology makes use of concrete material reality to engage the sacred. Before the advent of Soviet atheism in Eastern Europe, icons were ubiquitous, as easily found in the bedrooms of the tsar as in the lowliest peasant's hut; the meaning of an icon resides equally in expensive originals and self-produced copies. In this way, iconographic theology is accessible to everyone. Traditionally, icons are said to be written, rather than painted, evoking a comparison to language, with a system of grammar, style, and symbolism. But although highly stylized and symbolic, the language of iconography is firmly grounded in material reality. A traditional icon is made from natural elements: animal (egg yolk, glue, gelatin), vegetable (wood, oil, vinegar), and mineral (gold, stone/gesso, colours) that are fused by human hands, characterizing a faith in an ever-present Kingdom of God. The starkly stylized, unrealistic rendering of biblical narratives, figures, and events convey an altered perspective, a profound knowledge that the world is not simply as it appears, but that creation—in its totality—is irrevocably transformed because of the Incarnation.

Iconographic style implicitly conveys a transfigured reality and elicits, for the viewers versed in its language, a recognition of their participation in its meaning. Although the iconoclasts of the eighth and ninth centuries accused the tradition of engaging in idolatry, worshipping painted wood, the presence of icons to this day speaks of the enduring victory of the iconophiles who defended the value of this tradition.[15] The Eastern Christian does not bow before an icon to worship the wood, but rather venerates the reality recognized through the material substance. The ordinary material

---

14 Divinization/deification or *theosis* is the traditional Eastern Christian manner of speaking of humanity's purpose. For a standard introduction, see John Meyendorff, *Byzantine Theology: Historical Trends and Doctrinal Themes* (New York: Fordham University Press, 1974).

15 For an outline of the iconoclast controversy, see Meyendorff.

used to create the icon leads beyond itself to disclose Divine presence.[16] The human figures do not suggest a standardized form of physical perfection. The representation of body in iconography throughout the centuries has not reflected shifting cultural ideals of beauty. The divinized body that we encounter in the icons is so because it participates in created existence.

We have discussed how the North American obsession with conformity to a commercially contrived concept of a desirable body alienates people whose bodies cannot approximate the fashion trend. Ironically, the people labelled with difference who have been rejected from the mainstream may be those with the greatest power to confront existential humanity. Disability's foregrounding of our elemental physicality enhances understanding of our humanity, which in turn facilitates spiritual growth and divinization.

This deepened experience of embodiment creates a consciousness of self that extends to other. Encountering God through and in our bodies is not the end but only the beginning of the life process of striving to live as an icon of Christ. The theology of the Trinity illuminates relationships of reciprocity and interdependence, highlighted by experiences of disability.

As we have discussed earlier, Eastern iconography depicts the Triune God within the biblical narrative of Abraham and Sarah, who warmly entertain the three weary travelling strangers (Gen. 18:1), angels in disguise. The old couple's generous hospitality engenders the Hebrew nation (Gen. 18:18) into which the Son of God is born. Clearly, we may understand that to share one's home and to respond to the needs of others is a good thing. Although the *others* in this event portray the three persons of God, perceiving God as *needy* may seem theologically incongruous. In this way we are led to rethink prevalent notions of neediness and dependence. God's ostensible need could be seen as an offering of an opportunity for relationship for the givers—Sarah and Abraham. Their openness to this opportunity for human relationship results in divine communion and a consequent transformation of identity. Literally, they become more than they believed they could be, bearing a child and reconfiguring themselves

---

16 On the Eastern Christian understanding of the whole of creation imbued with the energies of God (which are God), see George Maloney, *A Theology of Uncreated Energies* (Milwaukee: Marquette University Press, 1978).

into a family. Their human possibilities expand through their profoundly human encounter with God. Significantly, as we learn further, beyond the iconographic account, the couple's encounter with divinity did not remove them from ordinary human existence. The story of Abraham and Sarah in Gerar (Gen. 20:1f.) suggests that they, in their relationships, were not exempt from struggles with deceit, doubt, and ambivalence.

Our contemporary pattern of social service provision in Western society, which generally manifests an unequal power relationship between a person with disability and a non-disabled person, fails to acknowledge the inherent reciprocity of human relationship. As we have emphasized throughout this volume, we need relationship to be human. Responding to others, sharing, interrelating is a human imperative. The mandatory interdependence and reciprocity involved in human relationships is exemplified by the three-person God. God, the ultimate perfection, is not an independent monad, but goes beyond self in order to be whole. The Trinity, in its kenotic love, necessarily spills over to other; it cannot be contained, but proceeds in a movement of self-emptying and therefore mutually fulfilling love (divine *perichoresis*).

By encountering God in our humanity, we are compelled to reach beyond ourselves to enfold all creation into the divine circle. Rejection or exclusion of others denies the divine reality. Variation in age, ability, or appearance is irrelevant, because the iconographic message emphasizes the transfigured meaning of matter, of "body." All of creation participates in the radical effect of Christ's embodiment and therefore all bodies, in their limitless variety, are equally valuable icons of God. Accommodation of each other's physicality is the vehicle through which we take part in divinization. Our humanity/divinity deepens and flourishes in human encounter, which flows in the Trinitarian paradigm of self through other.

In the icon of the Trinity, the image of the travellers/angels/God sitting down to a meal signifies the transformation of the fundamental human need for sustenance into a sacred event. The ordinary is also extraordinary when we seek to live as authentically as possible. By serving each other, by caring for our multifaceted bodies, by engaging in relationship, we become living icons, more human to be more like God. The circular outpouring of Trinitarian love is interrupted if any are alienated from community.

Christian community, in order to authentically reflect a Trinitarian ethos, *needs* to ceaselessly recreate itself by continually seeking deeper understanding of humanity in and through relationship. Hence, denying relationship is a rejection of God. Entering the Trinitarian paradigm, we seek the multi-variegated possibilities of humankind; we seek new understandings and experiences of embodiment that the minority in society, who manage to conform to ideas of bodily perfection, lack.

In the Christian East, Trinity is imprinted not only in liturgical texts of worship, but also on the bodies of the worshipping faithful. The sign of the cross is made with three fingers pressed together, and is repeated three times. Infants are plunged into baptismal water three times. Prayers are repeated thrice, as are prostrations and circumambulations. The physical body is integral to worship; the significance of the incarnated Triune God permeates sense, thought, and action. Not only sight, but hearing, smell, touch, and movement are actively engaged in liturgy. Even the hesychastic practice of the prayer of the heart is synchronized with the rhythmic intake and exhalation of breath. Bodily impairment cannot preclude participation in the rituals of faith. Breathing, therefore (even if with a respirator), becomes the only requirement for membership in the community of the faithful: in the life of the Trinity.

Observances of feast days and periods of fasting throughout the liturgical year involve ritual practices at home as well as in church. These provide a strong sense of continuity and belonging for the faithful, much like, for example, the Judaic Seder supper at Passover. Traditional Eastern Christian celebrations of Christmas are inextricably tied to the iconographic depiction of Christ's Nativity. The Slavic Nativity proper is repeated continually during the Christmas Eve Compline, as if to indelibly impress our consciousness with the momentous significance of the Incarnation: "God is with us; understand [take heed] all you peoples and be humbled, for God is with us!"

A common iconographic rendering of this unfathomable event contains the ambivalence inherent in embodiment: shadows of doubt, pain, inextricable from light and life. The central focus of the icon is a reclining figure of Mary, the mother of Christ. She is wrapped in a shroud, with only her face and one hand exposed. Her face rests on her hand in a posture of weariness; her expression is one of marked sorrow. Her body turns away from her child, conveying a grim impression of exhausted suffering. The infant lies in a coffin tightly swaddled in the cloth strips of burial—like an Egyptian mummy. A midwife and wet nurse are in attendance, washing the tiny naked, adult-looking child. Our contemplation of divine embodiment includes inescapable facets of corporeal being: the pain of childbirth, the service of the women, the vulnerability of the body held at the mercy of another, the suggestion of fear of the small figure turned towards the water but clinging to the woman's arm. In the opposite corner, a deeply troubled Joseph is being tempted to mistrust his wife and reject her purported innocence. Heaven, nature, humanity are witness to God become flesh. There is no room to doubt the ambivalence of this reality. Death permeates the scene of birth.

Mortality is a fact of embodiment. It is an ordinary human event and, like all that is fully human, it allows for transcendence, for deeper signification, since what is human leads to more than we can predetermine. A fear of mortality is among the myriad reasons attributed to the systemic rejection of people with disabilities in Western culture. The construct of disability, wrapped, as it has been for many generations, in the shroud of scientific professionalism has served as a screen onto which Western culture has projected spectres of pain, deviance, deficit, mutability, and mortality.[17] In contrast, the Nativity icon—and the Christmas rituals that accompany its theology—encompasses the reality of death and acknowledges a continuity of community that can mitigate the terror linked to mortality that is so prevalent in the Western world. The many symbolic elements of the ritual Christmas Eve meal or Holy Supper reinforce a belief in continuity with past and future generations. A place at the table is even left for those participants in the celebrations who have died. A candle in the window signals welcome to any wanderers. All must be included in Christian hospitality. The valuing of relationship even beyond death most adamantly, if perhaps absurdly, manifests the notion that reciprocity does not require a quantifiably equal response (in kind) from one party to another. The table itself becomes a metaphor for the Kingdom of God here on earth.

---

17 Wendell contends that a cultural fear of pain is "expressed or displaced as a fear of people with pain, which often isolates those with painful disabilities" (109).

We, regardless of ability, require communion with each other in order to reflect the Trinity through our humanity.

A brief mention of the icon of the Resurrection is in order, since it depicts the ultimate Christian notion of transcendence of life over death in Christ. Most salient to this reflection is that the Resurrection is a bodily one: the tortured, punctured, wounded body of Jesus Christ, God incarnate. The typical iconographic depiction represents the resurrected Christ firmly grasping the wrists of Adam and Eve in order to physically pull them from the grave. Because these two figures symbolize the sinfulness of the human condition, the iconographic action of Christ is revolutionary. Through Christ's Resurrection, human nature is no longer fallen; the body is not inherently the vehicle for sin. Human corporeal existence, in its endless variety, engages with God in time, in space, in matter.[18]

The association of disability with defect and sin cannot be supported in Eastern Christian theology. The iconographic theology of the Christian East also eschews elitism and mandates fully inclusive communities. Just as the disabled body is forced into a heightened awareness of embodiment, iconography facilitates a deepening of human experience. Ironically, the medieval self-flagellants mentioned earlier may have been unwittingly experiencing bodily transcendence. Their efforts to erase their physicality may, albeit unintentionally, have served to draw a greater awareness to their bodies through self-inflicted pain and discomfort. Far from manifesting the body and mind as exclusive realities, this hyper focus on body may have led to a transcendence that they interpreted as a state of grace beyond the "shackles" of corporeality. Generations of exposure to Soviet atheism, Western scholasticism, and mainstream media values has obscured much of the individual relevance of faith traditions, resulting in the transmogrification of iconography from theological source text and

---

18 In his renowned Easter homily, John Chrysostom addresses his listeners as labourers who have arrived at work at different times. Contrary to most valued work ethics, Chrysostom asserts that those who have completed a twelve-hour workday as well as those completing only one hour of work have reason to rejoice. Everyone receives equal payment (equal does not mean the same). Life is for the first and the last—in effect erasing the value attributed to the ability to accumulate wealth. Through Christ's resurrection, Chrysostom proclaims, death has lost its sting.

The text of the homily is accessible at http://www.ocf.org/features/EasterSermon.html (accessed August 27, 2012).

life guide to popular art form. Like the outcome of the Genesis encounter of the elderly couple with the Triune God in Genesis, a return to realities of embodiment through a Trinitarian paradigm bears the promise of abundant fruits.

When we all work towards truly inclusive communities, there is no telling how experiences of physicality lived by those of us with disability labels may contribute to the richness of our shared humanity. Consciously unlearning our enculturated disability prejudices by focusing on including people with disabilities into the heart of our churches offers a vital opportunity for renewal and conversion. A Trinitarian paradigm for understanding disability, whereby hitherto ignored and devalued embodied subjectivities are validated because Christ's Incarnation discloses God's presence among our interdependent human existence, is an imperative of our Christian inheritance. Only when our communities cease to participate in society's alienation of those who are labelled as too different, as disabled, will we be Christian communities—sanctuaries of our living God.

> The fundamental quality of human beings is to be in relationship ... It is in truly meeting the other that transformation starts. Here, individuals begin to discover what compassion really is and can come to rejoice in people and their differences. —Jean Vanier, "A Human Future"

12

Discovering Trinity in Disability

Disability studies has shed much light on the meaning of disability in cultures and societies. Recognizing how and why Western society has constructed both disability and normalcy as oppositional categories helps us begin to recognize and understand how and why we treat people who have disabilities the way we do. Once we distinguish the process of how society, in its institutionalized structures and enculturated prejudiced attitudes, disables people with anomalous bodies, we become aware of the learned behaviours we all perform to keep the difference of disability on the periphery of what we accept as ordinary. We are all complicit in perpetuating the oppressive status quo of mainstream normalcy regardless of dis/ability status, until we consciously work at unlearning habituated ways of thinking about difference.

Given that disability is a contingent category, historical studies require exceptional contextualizing. In seeking to trace responses to disability from before and since the Gospel era, we understand that we may be inappropriately imposing current perspectives onto the past. For this reason, we search for responses to people who are perceived as peripheral to established power (as people with various anomalies are today). We include references to identified impairments, illness, poverty, epilepsy (fits), and "otherness" of any sort. Retracing our tradition with attention to attitudes towards difference enables us to observe to what extent Christian practice approximates Christian teaching and ultimately to understand our present position and gauge our future trajectory. We have discovered that by highlighting disability, we uncover the profound link among the Incarnation, the Christian view of the nature of humanity, and our relationship with God.

Uncovering and encountering these connections has crystallized the imperative for communities to refresh their Christian mandate to vitalize the Kingdom of God here and now. A focus on disability in our sacred history suggests that truly inclusive community not only can liberate all members from the iron clench of the dictates of normalcy, which instills fear of human diversity, but also can enrich our immediate experience of our existential humanity. In short, we believe that inclusive communities enhance joy in all our lives.

From the Gospel example of Jesus' life and its interpretation by generations of disciples, we as Christians inherit a call to emulate Christ, to be Christ together in community. Our impulse to differentiate our communities from society at large may be more of a response to fear and anxiety about the increasing pluralism and diversity of contemporary society than an alternative to oppressive measures for those on the peripheries of society. Fear is more of a barrier to than a motivator towards the Kingdom. While mainstream fears of anomaly have modelled our segregated responses to people with disabilities, the call to be in and not of the world can be heard as a mandate not to retreat from the mainstream, but rather to transfigure it through the loving relationship of the Trinity.

Jesus' call to action is summarized in the Golden Rule: "You shall love the Lord your God with all your heart, and with all your soul, and with all your mind, and with all your strength … You shall love your neighbour as yourself" (Mk. 12:30-31). This echo of Deuteronomy 6:5 underpins the Christian's understanding of the enduring connection between faith and action: "the only thing that counts is faith working through love" (Gal. 5:6). This is key to our understanding of the distinction between charity, as it has developed in Western societies, and *caritas*, which we see as an extension of our recognition of being loved by God.

Pope Benedict reminds us, "Being Christian is not the result of an ethical choice or a lofty idea, but the encounter with an event, a person, which gives life a new horizon and a decisive direction" (1). The distinction between charity and *caritas* helps us appreciate Longmore's critique of institutionalized charitable activity via telethons that commodify disability as a tool for mollifying middle-class guilt of excessive self-gratifying consumption. This mechanism of giving provides therapy for selfishness through exhibitions of philanthropy directed at an invalidated population that promises to reform (become non-disabled) due to the generous donations of *successful* (wealthy) citizens. Charity in this way creates a power differential and belittles the receivers of alms. In contrast, *caritas* responds with compassion to the needs of equals, caring less for self than for the relief of another. We witness *caritas* in the early Church and in the development of monasticism. *Caritas* reaches out to others with humility and respect, mindful of every human being's dignity. *Caritas* demands that we take individual responsibility for our interaction with other people.

This personal responsibility might seem daunting: What am I to do? How am I to act? What if I say something offensive? Our discomfort may be well founded: we are being called into new interactions, new relationships. Change produces some level of fear. However, our conversion to *caritas* means opening ourselves to others, not as experts or professionals, but as loving human beings who turn to the other in the attitude and sincerity with which we would wish others to approach us. Once we proceed beyond our initial anxiety, *caritas* is liberating. Its strength conquers our fear and ushers us into relationships of endless potential where we not only meet ourselves, but within the process we meet our God.

When the spirit of *caritas* dominates our community, we create sanctuary. Sanctuary is not a hiding place from the mainstream, but a liminal space whereby the rules of the establishment are suspended to allow for continuous and unpredictable possibility. Our community based in *caritas* is the dwelling place of the living Christ; this sacred space is sanctuary.

All too often, Christian communities exist on foundations other than *caritas*, betraying instead patronizing self-righteousness. Christianity in early 20th-century Canada encapsulates this problem. Canadian churches, whose borders were defined by white, British notions of superiority, were involved in two horrendous social experiments in the name of Christ. Residential schools for Aboriginal children and eugenics programs were both promoted as a benevolent and scientific solution to social problems. Fear of difference threatened the complacency of a white British Christian establishment whose fear of the "menace of the feeble-minded," "the savage," "the yellow scare," and "the degenerate" was cloaked in a Christian discourse of virtuous charity and morality. Christian churches cooperated with the Canadian government in "facilitating" the education of Canada's First Nations. Today we recognize that what purported to be "Christian" education was in fact an imposition of white European values onto the Aboriginal population of Canada. Although we have no doubt that many of those involved in residential programs may have had good intentions, the very notion of uprooting children from their families, severing their contact with their families, and punishing them for expressing their inherited culture demonstrates forced homogeneity more than it celebrates and respects the diversity of God's creative love. An equally devastating social experiment, eugenics, targeted people with disabilities as the source of criminality and moral degeneracy in growing urban centres. The eugenics movement was a popular phenomenon in Western societies until Nazi Germany took the notion of eugenics to its logical conclusion: eliminating "undesirables" and nurturing the Master Race.

Respected Canadian Christians such as Emily Murphy, J.S. Woodsworth, William Aberhart, Ernest Manning, and even Tommy Douglas to a lesser or greater extent promoted eugenic policies, all in the name of building a Christian society.[19] Christian leaders conflated the Gospel call to evangelize with British imperialist ideology. The Social Gospel they ardently advanced ostensibly sought to create an equitable, moral, hard-working society—based on Christian values. The eugenic philosophy believed that criminality was genetically determined; for this

---

19 See such works as Alvin Finkel, *Social Policy and Practice in Canada: A History* (Waterloo: Wilfrid Laurier University Press, 2006); Jane Harris-Zsovan, *Eugenics and the Firewall: Canada's Dirty Little Secret* (Toronto: University of Toronto Press, 2010); Angus McLaren, *Our Own Master Race: Eugenics in Canada* (Toronto: McClelland and Stewart, 1990); Maria Truchan-Tataryn *(In)visible Images: Seeing Disability in Canadian Literature, 1823–1974* (Saarbrücken: LAP, 2011); J.S. Woodsworth, *Strangers Within Our Gates* (Toronto: University of Toronto Press, reprint, 1972).

reason, it was necessary to promote "good" genes, as it were, while preventing "bad" genes from reproducing.

"Good" genetic stock was believed to be evident—obvious, really—in economic success. The ramifications of the belief in this defective science remains a horrific segment of Western history, with reverberations reaching into our present day. In Canada, good Christian stock was measured by the privileged British establishment: white, wealthy, and healthy. The vast and varied populations immigrating to Canada to work in the burgeoning developments of the country had their humanity valued on a scale according to their ability to approximate middle-class British-ness. The more one differed in skin colour, language, dress, and habits, the more integrally defective one was considered to be by the authorities of political and cultural leadership—most saliently, leaders of and in Christian communities. Failure to appear middle-class British, or WASP (White Anglo-Saxon Protestant), suggested mental insufficiency, just as failure to appear physically fit implied inferior genetic makeup and resulted in the risk of sterilization. The infamous sterilization laws, which in some provinces provided a legal framework for the forced sterilization of people deemed unfit to breed, remained in force until the 1970s. Following the Nazi eugenic Holocaust and better science, the eugenic period has retreated into the shadows of history, perhaps as an embarrassing episode of hysteria brought on by fear of immigration shifts. Yet the reality of this fear of Other continues to haunt our societies with the oppressive attitudes and stigma directed towards people with disabilities. The mandate of normalcy still irrepressibly defines borders of desirability and acceptability. We still expect "those" types of people to have special places such as schools, homes, and centres—places where we do not have to see or interact with them unless we want some volunteer experience. Eugenic notions survive in advancing medical technologies of genetic engineering. Although it is no longer politically correct to say so, the sentiment of "better dead than disabled" still erodes the humanity of our societies.

In Canada, the Saskatchewan farmer Robert Latimer, who planned and executed the murder of his twelve-year-old daughter, Tracy, in 1993, received a lesser sentence for manslaughter rather than first-degree murder. To this day, Latimer has shown no remorse for the killing, claiming he acted out of love. He called the murder mercy killing. This man enjoys folk hero status; many Christian churches support him. Would we defend parents' right to murder their child because the child had chronic migraines, depression, or difficult behaviours? Tracy had cerebral palsy; her father ended her "pain" by ending her life. Robert Latimer has had an international stage on which to portray himself as a compassionate citizen. Yet Tracy's father not only claimed her life, but also her voice, her human status. Do we feel compassion for Tracy or for her burdened parent? When Tracy is portrayed as a body-in-pain (suffering flesh) in relation to her father—the hard-working family man—with whom should we relate? With whom would Jesus relate?

Our social institutions suggest that we sustain a prevailing desire for a homogeneity that reflects my own self as the average, as the mainstream norm. Thus, in the face of social fears of global unstable economies, political uncertainty, illegal migration, and the like, it seems that we succumb to fear of Other because by focusing on the Other as problem, deviant, or inadequate in some way, we permit ourselves to feel superior, normal, sufficient. This is the superior side of binary thinking, sufficiently ordinary so as not to be (thankfully) special!

By perpetuating the notion of disability as abnormality, we avoid encountering the realities of our human corporeality. Currently, we are witnessing a widespread trend towards social and political reforms that appeal to individual interests. We hear rhetoric that assures us that policies profiting the "average" voter's interests will profit everyone. While this rhetoric may win seats in Parliament, promoting the myth of middle-class normalcy merely perpetuates stratification and the social exclusion of everyone who cannot conform with money or surgery to requisite being. Instead of reaching for a fabricated one-size-fits-all solution, we need to be aware of the diversity through which we come to recognize God's ecstatic love. We need to acknowledge each of us as participating in natural human diversity and thereby experience the consequence of this unity in diversity as the presence of Christ. Letting go of the comforts of mainstream normalcy, we can be free to follow in Jesus' footsteps into Trinity.

Thus we return to the Trinity—God who is community. We who are created in that image, and the creation that is the gift of God, find our origin in that divine relationship. Divine love is shared mutually and equally among the three persons, yet that love is so overwhelming and borderless that it consciously goes into nothingness and creates. The icon of the Trinity opens up and calls the observer(s) into the relationship. So we are all participants in that ceaseless flow of love. Although this truth has been held firmly throughout two millennia of Christian witness, it is a difficult truth to activate in life. Yet it is neither romantic nor utopic. People of faith throughout history have lived the Trinitarian paradigm and demonstrated that humans can overcome sin—both personal and social. They have demonstrated that we can overcome our fear of those who are different and can recognize that growing in our relatedness with others, especially those who are markedly different from us, is life giving. The life to which we open ourselves is expansive and unfathomable in its fullness, because it is the divine life: the life of the Trinity.

The Trinitarian paradigm, which we proffer as a necessary framework to revitalize the Christian Church, is as old as Christianity itself. The early Church conveys an understanding of the sacredness of recognizing our most profound humanity, which discloses our fundamental interconnection with all creation. In turn, this admission and appreciation of our corporeality and our shared experience of humanity with Christ illuminates the mission of Jesus' life. Christians in the early Church emulated his radical example of relationship with the disenfranchised of any population. Sharing their humanity, connecting with the humanity of others, was a natural outpouring of the relationship they actively held with God: Jesus (the incarnate Son), Father, and Spirit. The outreach of the early Church communities was a response to dwelling in the Sanctuary—the place of God. The wonder with which non-Christians documented these initial Christian communities attests to the palpable joy and love they revealed.

We have traced this understanding of the Christian imperative to inclusive community throughout our sacred heritage, from the Gospels to our own time. We have looked back to our biblical roots to illustrate the source of (mis)conceptions about our faith's responses to human corporeal diversity that still circulate today. We have uncovered a significant thread of inclusive Trinitarian community weaving throughout the tapestry of our sacred history. We hope that revealing this thread will be the beginning of ever-greater revelations of the living presence of God in our enfleshed world.

We know from the example of Christ's followers for two millennia that re-visioning our humanity through the Incarnation entails a conscious interrogation of constructs of normalcy and deviance so that we can recognize our connection to other human beings, honouring their unknowable difference as we honour our own differences, too. We know that reaching out in a Trinitarian example of inclusivity will generate fear, anxiety, and possibly ridicule, but we stand with Christ, at once creating and entering sanctuary. Suffering, illness, and impairment can be treated, endured, and ameliorated, as long as people are enveloped in caring, support, respect, and love. We journey through our fears not by avoiding them, but rather by following Christ's call and accepting the strength of the Holy Spirit so we can move beyond charity to *caritas*; so we can oppose habitual institutionalization of people of whom we are afraid; so we can let go of our desire to protect our own individual interests and recognize that our interests are best served when we emulate the Trinity. Living Trinity, living diversity, living connectedness with humanity is life's fullness. As we come to understand the impact of the Trinitarian example of being and specifically of being Christian, no one would be relegated to the hallways, away from the party, as we saw in our introductory scene. We would contribute our humanity in all its uniqueness to the ceaseless circle of relationship that we observe in the icon of hospitality—the Trinity.

> Our experience of disability must be embraced in order for there to be the creation of a new meaning of life. (Overboe, 84)

Bibliography

Abrams, Judith Z. *Judaism and Disability: Portrayals in Ancient Texts from the Tanach through the Bavli.* Washington, D.C.: Gallauder University Press, 1998.

Anderson, Bernhard W. *Understanding the Old Testament.* Third edition. Englewood Cliffs, N.J.: Prentice Hall, 1975.

Athanasius. "On the Incarnation." *Nicene and Post-Nicene Fathers. Volume 4. Athanasius: Select Works and Letters. Second Series.* Peabody, Mass.: Hendrickson, 1995.

Aumann, Jordan. *Christian Spirituality in the Catholic Tradition.* London: Sheed & Ward, 1985.

Ayres, Lewis. "The Fundamental Grammar of Augustine's Trinitarian Theology." In *Augustine and His Critics*, eds. Robert Dodaro and George Lawless. London: Routledge, 2000.

Baptism, Eucharist, and Ministry. Faith and Order Paper No. 111. Geneva: World Council of Churches, 1982. http://www.oikoumene.org/fileadmin/files/wcc-main/documents/p2/FO1982_111_en.pdf

Benedict XVI, *Deus Caritas Est.* Vatican City: Libreria Editrice Vaticana, 2005. http://www.vatican.va/holy_father/benedict_xvi/encyclicals/documents/hf_ben-xvi_enc_20051225_deus-caritas-est_en.html

Bornkamm, Gunther, Gerhard Barth, and Heinz Joachim Held. *Tradition and Interpretation in Matthew.* Philadelphia: Westminster Press, 1963.

Brown, Raymond E. *New Testament Essays.* New York: Paulist Press, 1965.

Chrysostom, John. "Homily XIV: 1 Timothy v. 8." *Nicene and Post-Nicene Fathers. Volume 13. Chrysostom: Homilies on Galatians, Ephesians, Philippians, Colossians, Thessalonians, Timothy, Titus, and Philemon. First Series.* Peabody, Mass.: Hendrickson, 1995.

Cook, Joan E. *Hear, O Heavens and Listen, O Earth: An Introduction to the Prophets.* Collegeville: Liturgical Press, 2006.

Cooper, Adam G. *The Body in St. Maximus the Confessor: Holy Flesh, Wholly Deified.* Oxford: Oxford University Press, 2005.

Coote, Robert. "The Meaning of the Name Israel." *The Harvard Theological Review* 65 (1972): 137–142.

Crislip, Andrew T. *From Monastery to Hospital: Christian Monasticism & the Transformation of Health Care in Late Antiquity.* Ann Arbor: University of Michigan Press, 2005.

Cusack, Carole M. "*Graciosi*: Medieval Christian Attitudes to Disability." *Disability and Rehabilitation* 19 (1997): 414–419.

Desroches, Leonard. *Love of Enemy: The Cross and Sword Trial.* Ottawa: Éditions Dunamis, 2002.

"Didache." In *The New Testament and Other Early Christian Writings*, ed. Bart D. Ehrman. London: Oxford University Press, 1998.

Ehrman, Bart D., ed. *The New Testament and Other Early Christian Writings.* London: Oxford University Press, 1998.

Eisland, Nancy. *The Disabled God: Towards a Liberatory Theology of Disability.* Nashville: Abingdon, 1995.

Garland Thomson, Rosemarie. *Extraordinary Bodies: Figuring Physical Disability in American Culture and Literature.* New York: Columbia University Press, 1997.

———. "Speaking About the Unspeakable: The Representation of Disability as Stigma in Toni Morrison's Novels." In *Courage and Tools: The Florence Howe Award for Feminist Scholarship, 1974–89*, eds. J. Glasgow and A. Ingram. New York: MLA Press, 1990. 238–251.

Goldstein, Jackie L. and Marc M. L. Godemont. "The Legend and Lessons of Geel, Belgium: A 1500-Year-Old Legend, a 21st-Century Model." *Community Mental Health Journal* 39 (2003): 441–458.

Gregory of Nazianzus. "To Cledonius." *Nicene and Post-Nicene Fathers. Volume 7. Cyril of Jerusalem, Gregory Nazianzen. Second Series.* Peabody, Mass.: Hendrickson, 1995.

Gregory of Nyssa. *From Glory to Glory: Texts from Gregory of Nyssa's Mystical Writings*, Introduction by Jean Daniélou, trans. and ed. Herbert Musurillo. Crestwood, N.Y.: St. Vladimir's Seminary Press, 1979.

Grillmeier, Aloys. *Christ in Christian Tradition, Volume One: From the Apostolic Age to Chalcedon (451).* Second revised edition. Oxford: Mowbrays, 1975.

Groce, Nora Ellen. *Everyone Here Spoke Sign Language: Hereditary Deafness on Martha's Vineyard.* Cambridge, Mass.: Harvard University Press, 1985.

Groce, Nora and Jessica Scheer. "Impairment as a Human Constant: Cross-Cultural and Historical Perspectives on Variation." *Journal of Social Issues*, 44 (1988): 23–37.

Gunton, Colin. "Augustine, the Trinity and the Theological Crisis of the West." *Scottish Journal of Theology* 43 (1990): 33–58.

Holman, Susan R. *The Hungry Are Dying: Beggars and Bishops in Roman Cappadocia.* Oxford: Oxford University Press, 2001.

Ignatius of Antioch. "To the Trallians." *Ante-Nicene Fathers. Volume 1. The Apostolic Fathers, Justin Martyr, Irenaeus.* Peabody, Mass.: Hendrickson, 1995.

Illich, Ivan. *The Rivers of the Future: The Testament of Ivan Illich*, ed. David Cayley. Toronto: Anansi, 2005.

Irenaeus of Lyons. "Against Heresies. Book II." *Ante-Nicene Fathers. Volume 1. The Apostolic Fathers, Justin Martyr, Irenaeus.* Peabody, Mass.: Hendrickson, 1995.

Kanner, L. *A History of the Care and Study of the Mentally Retarded*. Springfield, Ill.: Charles C. Thomas, 1964.

Karam, Cyril. "Saint Basil on the Holy Spirit—Some Aspects of His Theology." *Word and Spirit* 1 (1979): 137–164.

Kasper, Walter. *Jesus the Christ*. New York: Paulist Press, 1976.

Khaled, Anatolios. *Athanasius*. London: Routledge, 2004.

Linton, Simi. *Claiming Disability: Knowledge and Identity*. New York: New York University Press, 1998.

Longmore, Paul K. "Conspicuous Contribution and American Cultural Dilemmas: Telethon Rituals of Cleansing and Renewal." In *The Body and Physical Difference: Discourses of Disability*, eds. David T. Mitchell and Sharon L. Snyders. Ann Arbor: University of Michigan Press, 1997. 134–158.

Louth, Andrew. "The Cappadocians." In *The Study of Spirituality*, eds. Cheslyn Jones, Geoffrey Wainwright and Edward Yarnold. Oxford: Oxford University Press, 1986. 161–168.

Luther, Martin. *Table Talk*, ed. and trans. Theodore G. Tappert in *Luther's Works. Volume 54*. Philadelphia: Fortress Press, 1967. 53.

Maloney, George. *A Theology of Uncreated Energies*. Milwaukee: Marquette University Press, 1978.

McDonald, H.D. "Development and Christology." *Vox Evangelica* 9 (1975): 5-27.

Melito of Sardis. "On the Nature of Christ". Fragment. *Ante-Nicene Fathers. Volume 8. The Twelve Patriarchs, Excerpts and Epistles, The Clementina, Apocrypha, Decretals, Memoirs of Edessa and Syriac Documents, Remains of the First Ages*. Peabody, Mass.: Hendrickson, 1995.

Meyendorff, John. *Byzantine Theology: Historical Trends and Doctrinal Themes*. New York: Fordham University Press, 1974.

Miccoli, Giovanni. "Théologie de la vie monastique chez Saint Pierre Damien (1007–1072)." *Théologie de La Vie Monastique: Études sur la Tradition Patristique*. Aubier, 1961. 459–483.

Murphy, Robert. *The Body Silent*. New York: Norton, 1990.

New Oxford Annotated Bible. Third edition. Oxford: Oxford University Press, 2001.

Oliver, Michael. *The Politics of Disablement: Critical Texts in Social Work and the Welfare State*. London: MacMillan, 1990.

Overboe, James. " 'Difference in Itself':Validating Disabled People's Lived Experience." In *Rethinking Normalcy: A Disability Studies Reader*, eds. Tanya Titchkosky and Rod Michalko. Toronto: Canadian Scholars' Press Inc., 2009. 75-87.

Oxford Dictionary of Current English. Third edition, ed. Catherine Soanes. Oxford: Oxford University Press, 2001.

Paphnutius. *Histories of the Monks of Upper Egypt & the Life of Onnophrius*, Introduction by and trans. Tim Vivian. Kalamazoo: Cistercian Publications, 1993.

Parsons, Mikeal C. "The Character of the Lame Man in Acts 3-4." *Journal of Biblical Literature* 124 (2005): 295–312.

Pelikan, Jaroslav. *Christianity and Classical Culture: The Metamorphosis of Natural Theology in the Christian Encounter with Hellenism.* New Haven: Yale University Press, 1993.

———. *The Christian Tradition. A History of the Development of Doctrine. Volume I. The Emergence of the Catholic Tradition (100–600).* Chicago: University of Chicago Press, 1971.

Rousseau, Philip. *Pachomius: The Making of a Community in Fourth-Century Egypt.* Berkeley: University of California Press, 1999.

Saward, John. "The Fool for Christ's Sake in Monasticism, East and West." In *Theology and Prayer*, ed. A.M. Allchin. Oxford: Fellowship of St. Alban and St. Sergius, 1975. 29–55.

Schmemann, Alexander. *Introduction to Liturgical Theology.* New York: St. Vladimir's Seminary Press, 1975.

Schönborn, Christoph. *God's Human Face: The Christ Icon.* San Francisco: Ignatius Press, 1994.

Schüsler Fiorenza, Elisabeth. *Jesus: Miriam's Child, Sophia's Prophet.* New York: Continuum, 1995.

Sheldrake, Philip. *Spaces for the Sacred: Place, Memory, and Identity.* Baltimore: Johns Hopkins University Press, 2001.

Sherwood, Polycarp, trans. *St. Maximus the Confessor. The Ascetic Life, The Four Centuries on Charity.* Ancient Christian Writers, No. 21. New York: Newman Press, 1955.

Socrates. "Ecclesiastical Histories." *Nicene and Post-Nicene Fathers. Volume 2. Socrates, Souzomenus: Church Histories. Second Series.* Peabody, Mass.: Hendrickson, 1995.

Stainton, Tim. "Reason, Grace and Charity: Augustine and the Impact of Church Doctrine on the Construction of Intellectual Disability." *Disability & Society* 23 (2008): 485–496.

Stiker, Henri-Jacques. *A History of Disability.* Ann Arbor: University of Michigan Press, 1999.

Tertullian. "Apologetic." *Ante-Nicene Fathers. Volume 3. Latin Christianity: Its Founder, Tertullian I. Apologetic; II. Anti-Marcion; III. Ethical.* Peabody, Mass.: Hendrickson, 1995.

———. "On Baptism." *Ante-Nicene Fathers. Volume 3. Latin Christianity: Its Founder, Tertullian I. Apologetic; II. Anti-Marcion; III. Ethical.* Peabody, Mass.: Hendrickson, 1995.

Thunberg, Lars. *Man and the Cosmos: The Vision of St. Maximus the Confessor.* Crestwood, N.Y.: St. Vladimir's Theological Seminary Press, 1985.

Titchkosky, Tanya. *Disability, Self, and Society*. Toronto: University of Toronto Press, 2003.

Truchan-Tataryn, Maria. *Benjy Resurrected: A Deconstruction of the Idiot in Faulkner's "The Sound and the Fury": A Thesis*. Saskatoon: University of Saskatchewan, 1999.

———. "In the Image of the Idiot: Reclaiming Human Suffering." *Religious Studies and Theology*. 19 #2 (2000): 70–91.

———. *(In)Visible Images: Seeing Disability in Canadian Literature, 1823–1974*. Saarbrücken: LAP, 2011.

Torrance, T.F. "The Place of Christology in Biblical and Dogmatic Theology." In *Essays in Christology for Karl Barth,* ed. T.H.L. Parker, 1956.

Tugwell, Simon. "The Dominicans." In *The Study of Spirituality*, eds. Cheslyn Jones, Geoffrey Wainwright and Edward Yarnold. Oxford: Oxford University Press, 1986. 296–300.

Vanier, Jean. "A Human Future: On Building a Compassionate Society." Cited in *A Human Future: A Thought Sheet for Canadians* 1 (2002) #1: 3.

———. *Community & Growth: Our Pilgrimage Together*. Toronto: Griffin House, 1979.

Ware, Kallistos. "The Fool in Christ as Prophet and Apostle." *Sobornost* 6, #2 (1984): 6–28.

———. "The Human Person as an Icon of the Trinity." *Sobornost* 8, #2 (1986): 6–23.

———. "Silence in Prayer: The Meaning of Hesychia." In *Theology and Prayer*, ed. A.M. Allchin. Oxford: Fellowship of St. Alban and St. Sergius, 1975. 8–28.

Wendell, Susan. *The Rejected Body: Feminist Philosophical Reflections on Disability*. New York: Routledge, 1996.

Williams, Rowan. "Sapientia and the Trinity: Reflection on the *De Trinitate*." In *Collectanea Augustiniana: Mélanges T. J. Van Bavel*, eds. B. Bruning, M. Lamberigts and J. van Houtem. Leuven: Leuven University Press, 1990. 317–332.

Winzer, Margaret A. "Disability and Society Before the Eighteenth Century." In *The Disability Studies Reader*, ed. Lennard J. Davis. New York: Routledge, 1997. 75–109.

World Report on Disability. Geneva: World Health Organization, 2011. http://www.who.int/disabilities/world_report/en/index.html

Yong, Amos. *Theology and Down Syndrome: Reimagining Disability in Late Modernity*. Waco, Tex.: Baylor University Press, 2007.

Young, Frances M. *Brokenness & Blessing: Towards a Biblical Spirituality*. Grand Rapids, Minn.: Baker, 2007.

Young, Iris Marion. *Justice and Politics of Difference*. Princeton: Princeton University Press, 1990.

Zizioulas, John D. *The Community of Being: Studies in Personhood and the Church*. Crestwood, N.Y.: St. Vladimir's Seminary Press, 1985.